OPERATIONS RESEARCH

OPERATIONS RESEARCH

Question Bank

N.V.R. Naidu
Professor & Head
Industrial Engineering and Management Department,
M.S. Ramaiah Institute of Technology, Bangalore

K.M. Babu
Vice Principal, Professor & Head
Industrial Engineering and Management Department,
BMS College of Engineering, Bangalore

G. Rajendra
Asst. Professor & Head
Industrial Engineering & Management Department,
Dr. Ambedkar Institute of Technology, Bangalore

I.K. International Publishing House Pvt. Ltd.
NEW DELHI • BANGALORE

Published by

I.K. International Publishing House Pvt. Ltd.
S-25, Green Park Extension, Uphaar Cinema Market
New Delhi - 110 016 (India)
E-mail : ik_in@vsnl.net

ISBN 978-81-89866-42-6

10 9 8 7 6 5 4 3

Published by Krishan Makhijani for I.K. International Publishing House Pvt. Ltd., S-25, Green Park Extension, Uphaar Cinema Market, New Delhi - 110 016 and Printed by Rekha Printers Pvt. Ltd., Okhla Industrial Area, Phase II, New Delhi - 110 020.

This book is dedicated to the

Lotus feet of

Lord Venkateshwara

and to our beloved parents

Preface

Operations research has emerged as the most spectacular aspect of optimization techniques. This book covers the introduction for each chapter and various questions. Practising professionals usually rate Operations Research as one of the most useful subjects studied in college.

This book provides the importance of each aspect and various problems of real situations in the organizations as well as in daily life.

The book consists of 12 chapters.

Chapters 1 to 4 consist of Linear programming problems, Graphically simplex method, Big M Method, Duality and Dual simplex method, which show the effective utilization of resources in the organization.

Chapter 5: **Transportation** provides to reach destination at minimum cost.

Chapter 6: **Assignment** provides the information to assign the work to machines or people.

Chapter 7: **Queuing problems** is useful for what time it takes to finish the job or customers.

Chapter 8: **Game theory** shows the probability of achievement.

Chapter 9: **Replacement and inventory management** provides the information of optimum time to replace that equipment and to manage the investment.

Chapter 10: **Replacement** determines when the machine or the equipment should be replaced.

Chapter 11: **Inventory management** problems helps in making decision of investment among alternatives.

Chapter 12: **Sequencing** shows the path which job to start in the beginning of a product.

NVR Naidu
KM Babu
G Rajendra

Contents

Preface *vii*

Authors *xi*

1. Linear Programming Problems 1-26
2. Graphically and Simplex Problems 27-34
3. Big M Method Problems 35-41
4. Duality and Dual Simplex Problems 42-57
5. Transportation Problems 58-87
6. Assignment Problems 88-109
7. Queuing Systems Problems 110-123
8. Project Management Problems 124-146
9. Game Theory Problems 147-156
10. Replacement Problems 157-163
11. Inventory Management Problems 164-170
12. Sequencing Problems 171-180

Authors

NVR Naidu graduated in Mechanical Engineering and did Post-graduation and Doctorial in Industrial Engineering at Sri Venkateswara University, Tirupati. Currently, he is a professor in Industrial Engineering and Management at M.S. Ramaiah Institute of Technology, Bangalore. He has 24 years of experience in teaching. He has presented/published 24 papers in various national and international conferences and referred journals. He has authored *Production and Operations Management, Metrology and Quality Control* and *Industrial Management.* He has guided about 50 live UG projects in the field of Production, Industrial Engineering and Management. Currently he is guiding three Ph.D. Students. He is a member of professional bodies like ORSI, ISTE, ISI, NIQR and IIE.

KM Babu is currently the Vice Principal and Prof. & Head of Industrial Engineering Management department, BMS College of Engineering, Bangalore. He has 20 years teaching experience. He has obtained his B.E., M.E. and Ph.D. degree from Bangalore University, Bangalore. He has presented/published 18 papers in various national and international conferences and referred journals. He has authored three textbooks for the engineering students. He has guided several UG projects for engineering students. Currently, he is guiding about five students for Ph.D. and MSc. (Engineering). He is a member of several professional bodies.

G. Rajendra is currently Assistant Professor & Head in the department of Industrial Engineering and Management, Dr. Ambedkar Institute of Technology, Bangalore. He has 21 years of teaching experience. He has obtained his B.E., M.E. from Bangalore University, Bangalore. He has presented/published five papers in national and international conferences. He has guided 25 UG projects in the field of Production, Industrial Engineering and Management. Currently he is pursuing Ph.D. at VTU, Belgaum, Karnataka. He has authored two Mechanical Engineering books for VTU syllabus and one in Human Resource Management for V semester Industrial Engineering and Management. He is a member of several professional bodies like ISTE, ISAMPE and IIE.

1

Linear Programming Problems

INTRODUCTION

The development of linear programming has been ranked among the most important scientific advances in the year 1930s. Its impact since 1950 has been extraordinary. Till today it has saved many thousands or millions of rupees for most companies or business houses in the various industrialized countries of the world. A major portion of all scientific computations on computers is devoted to the use of linear programming. The programming problems in general are concerned with the use of allocation of scarce resources such as labour, materials, machines and capital in the best possible manner so that the costs are minimized and profits are maximized.

The term linear programming defines a particular class of programming problems that meet the following conditions:

The decision variables involved in the problem are non-negative i.e. positive or zero in nature, the function is normally referred to as the objective function. The operating rule governing the process can be expressed as a set of linear equations or inequalities. This set is referred to as the constraint set.

Linear programming technique is widely used to solve a number of military, economic, industrial and social problems. The primary reasons for its wide use are that a large variety of problems in diverse fields can be represented by it. Efficient techniques for solving linear programming problems are available, ease through which data variations can be handled through linear programming models.

Any problem whose mathematical model fits the general format of the linear programming model can be solved efficiently by simple method, size is no matter. There are some reasons for the tremendous impact of linear programming in recent decades.

Two-variable linear programming model deals with the graphical solution. Though two-variable problems hardly exist in practice, the treatment provides concrete ideas for the development of the general solution algorithm.

The graphical method shows that the optimum linear programming solution is always associated with a corner point of the solution space. The results are key to the development of the general algebraic simple method for solving any LP model. A main feature of the simple method is that it solves the LP in iterations. Each iteration moves the solution to a new corner point that has the potential to improve the value of the objective function.

Applications

- Optimizing refinery operations.
- Supply distribution marketing (SDM) system.
- Diet problem.
- Work scheduling problem.
- Capital budgeting problem.
- Short-term financial planning.
- Blending problems.
- Productions process models.
- Inventory model.

Linear Programming Problems

1. A firm products A, B, C and D. There are four operators (I, II, III and IV), who are capable of producing any of these products. The processing time varies from operator to operator. The firm records 8 hours of working per day and allows 30 minutes for lunch. The products A, B, C and D give a profit of Rs. 8, 6, 5 and 4 per product respectively. The processing time for each product is given below. Find the optimum distribution schedule to maximize profit.

	Products (processing time in minutes)			
Operators	**A**	**B**	**C**	**D**
I	15	9	10	6
II	10	6	9	6
III	25	15	15	9
IV	15	9	10	10

2. A boat manufacturer builds two types of boats: type A and type B. The boats built during the months of January-June go on sale in the months July-December at a profit of Rs. 2000/- per type A boat and Rs. 1500/- per type B boat. Those built during the months July-December go on sale in the months January-June at a profit of Rs. 4000/- per type A boat and Rs. 3300/- per type B boat. Each type A boat requires 5 hours in the carpentry shop and 3 hours in the finishing shop. Each type B boat requires 8 hours in the carpentry shop and 11 hours in the finishing shop. During each half year period a maximum of 12,000 hours and 15,000 hours are available in the carpentry and finishing shops respectively. Sufficient material is available to build more than 3000 type A boats and 3000 type B boats a year. How many of each type of boats should be built during each half year in order to maximize the profit. Formulate as an LPP.

3. A student has two final exams to prepare for. Each hour of study he devotes to course A is expected to return him Rs. 600 in terms of long range benefits and each hour of study he devotes to course B is expected to return him Rs. 300 in terms of long range benefits. The shops are all closed; the student has only 15 chocolates remaining. He feels he needs one chocolate every 20 minutes while studying for course B and 1 for every 12 minutes while studying for course A. Time is running short and only 4 hours remain to prepare for exam. It is necessary that the student must devote at least 2 hours for studying. The student would like to maximize his returns for the effort expended. Solve this problem as an LPP and determine optimum policy for the student by solving the problem.

4. A manufacturer of packing material manufacturing two types of packing tins—round and flat. Major production facilities involved are cutting and joining. The cutting department can process 300 round tins or 500 flat tins per hour. The joining department can process 400 round tins and 300 flat tins per hour. If the profit contribution of round tins is Rs. 100 per tin and that of flat is Rs. 80 per tin. Formulate the problem as an LPP.

5. Consider a small plant which makes two types of automobile parts say A and B. The plant buys castings from a supplier. Castings for part A costs Rs. 2 each and casting for part B costs Rs. 3 each. The castings are machined, bored and polished. The details of machining capacity and running costs of the machines are as follows:

Machine	Capacity in pieces per hour		Running cost (Rs. per hour)
	Part A	Part B	
Lathe	25	40	20
Boring	28	35	14
Polishing	35	25	17.50
Selling price/unit	Rs. 5	Rs. 6	

The table above also indicates the selling price for the two parts. Assuming that any combination of part A and part B can be sold in the market, determine the optimal product mix. Formulate the above as an LPP and solve. *(Mech. Mar. 2001, IEM 2000)*

6. A company is trying to determine the correct blend of 2 types of feed. Both contain various percentages of four essential ingredients as shown below:

Ingredient	Percentage per kg of feed		Minimum required/kg
	Feed I	Feed II	
1	40	30	5
2	10	30	2
3	20	40	4
4	40	10	6

If feed I costs Rs. 50 per kg and feed II costs Rs. 40 per kg, determine the least cost blend.

7. A reputed computer center offers two kinds of services to its customers, namely, "regular service" and "special service". Each hour spent on "regular service" brings in a contribution of Rs. 250 and the contribution per hour for "special services" is Rs. 500. The "special service" only requires the deployment of skilled programmers and a maximum of 100 hours per week of programmers' 'time is available to the center. Both the services require computing time and a maximum of 400 hours of computing time is available per week. The hourly operational costs for "regular" and "special" services are Rs. 100 and Rs. 250 respectively. The weekly budget for meeting the operating expense is Rs. 80,000. In order that center's market share for the "regular service" be maintained the center has to allot minimum of 200 hours/week for "regular service". How should the center allot time for two services, so as to maximize the total contribution to the concern?

8. A farmer owns 200 pigs that consume 90 kg of special feed daily. The feed is a mixture of corn and soybean meal with the following compositions.

Feed	Kgs/kg of feed stuff			Cost (Rs./kg)
	Calcium	Protein	Fiber	
Corn	0.001	0.09	0.02	2
Soybean	0.002	0.6	0.06	6

The daily dietary requirements of the pigs are:

- At most 1% calcium.
- At least 30% protein.
- At most 5% fiber.

Determine the daily minimum cost of the feed mix.

9. A firm manufactures headache pills in 2 sizes A and B. Size A contains 2 grains of aspirin, as 5 grains of bicarbonate and 1 grain of codeine. Size B contains 1 grain of aspirin, 8 grains of bicarbonate and 6 grains of codeine. Users find that it requires at least 12 grains of aspirin, 74 grains of bicarbonate and 24 grains of codeine for providing immediate effect if required to determine the least number of pills a patient should take to get immediate relief. Formulate as an LP model.

10. Two products are manufactured by passing sequentially through 3 machines. Time per m/c allocated to the two products is limited to 10 hrs/day. Find the optimal product mix if the production time and profit/unit of each product is as follows:

	Production time (minutes/unit)			
Product	**m/c I**	**m/c II**	**m/c III**	**Profit (Rs./unit)**
A	10	6	8	20
B	5	20	15	30

11. A TV company operates two assembly lines: line I and line II. Each line is used to assemble the components of three types of TV's—colour, standard and economy. The expected daily production on each line is as follows:

TV model	Line I	Line II
Colour	3	1
Standard	1	1
Economy	2	6

The daily running costs for two lines averages Rs. 6000 for line I and Rs. 4000 for line II. It is given at least 24 colour, 16 standard and 48 economy TV sets for which an order is pending. Formulate and solve the above LPP.

12. The manager of an oil refinery has to decide upon the optimal mix of two possible blending processes of which the inputs and outputs per production run are as follows:

Process	Input		Output	
	Crude A	Crude B	Gasoline X	Gasoline Y
1	5	3	5	8
2	4	5	4	4

The maximum amounts available of crude A and B are 200 units and 150 units respectively. Market requirement shows that at least 100 units of gasoline X and 80 units of gasoline Y must be produced. The profits per production run from process 1 and process 2 are Rs. 30 and Rs. 40 respectively. Formulate the LPP and solve graphically.

13. A person requires 10, 12 and 12 units of chemicals A, B and C respectively for his garden. A liquid product contains 5, 2 and 1 units of A, B and C per bottle. A dry product contains 1, 2 and 4 units of A, B and C per carton. If the liquid product costs Rs. 30 per bottle and the dry product costs Rs. 20 per carton, how many of each should be purchased in order to minimize the cost and meet the requirements.

14. A full service facility for a loan policy involving a maximum fund of Rs. 12 crore is in the process of being formulated at the IDBI Bank. The following table provides pertinent data about different types of loans and the interest rates. Bad debts are unrecovered and hence produce no interest revenue. Competition with other financial institutions of the area requires the bank to allocate at least 40% of the funds to farm and commercial loans. To assist housing industry in the region, home loans must be equal to least 50% of the personal, car, and home loans. The bank also has stated policy specifying that the overall ratio for bad debts on all loans may not exceed 0.04. Formulate linear programming problem for the above.

Type of loan	Interest rate	Probability of bad debt
Personal	0.14	0.10
Car	0.13	0.07
Home	0.12	0.03
Farm	0.125	0.05
Commercial	0.10	0.02

15. A manufacturer produces 3 products A, B and C. Each product can be produced on one of two machines I and II. The time required for one unit of each product on a machine is given below:

Product	Time to produce Hrs/units	
	Machine I	Machine II
A	0.5	0.6
B	0.7	0.8
C	0.9	1.05

16. There are 85 hrs available on each machine. The operating cost is Rs. 5/hrs for m/c I and Rs. 4/hr for m/c II and requirements are at least 90 units of A, at least 80 units of B and at least 60 units of C. The manufacturer wishes to meet the requirement at minimum cost. Formulate as an LPP and solve. *(EE, EC Aug. 2002)*

17. An advertising company wishes to plan an advertising campaign in three different media—TV, radio and magazines. The purpose of the advertising program is to reach as many potential customers as possible. Results of a market study are given below:

	Television		Radio	Magazine
	Day time	Prime time		
Cost of advertising unit Rs.	40,000	75,000	30,000	15,000
No. of potential customers reached/unit	400,000	900,000	500,000	200,000
No. of women customers reached/unit	300,000	400,000	200,000	100,000

The company does not want to spend more than Rs. 800,000 on advertising. It further requires that:

- At least 2 million exposures take place among women.
- Advertising on television be limited to Rs. 500,000.
- At least 3 advertising units be brought on day time television and 2 units during prime time.
- The number of advertising units on radio and magazine should each be between 5 and 10.

Formulate the above problem as an LPP.

18. A manufacturer produces two types of products A and B. Each product can be produced on any one of the two machines M_1 and M_2. The time required to produce one unit of each product is:

Product	Time to produce machine M_1	One unit (hours) Machine M_2
A	2	6
B	5	3

Machine M_1 can work for 100 hours per week and M_2 for 180 hours per week. The operating costs of the machines are Rs. 30/- per hour and Rs. 40/- per hour respectively. The market requirements are that, at least 30 units of A and 40 units of B be produced per week. Formulate the LPP and determine the number of products of type A and type B to be produced per week.

19. A used car dealer wishes to stock up his lot to maximize his profit. He can select cars A, B and C which are valued wholesale at Rs. 5,000, Rs. 7, 000 and Rs. 8000 respectively. These can be sold at Rs. 6,000, Rs. 8,500 and Rs. 10,500 respectively. For each car type the probabilities of sales are:

Type of car	A	B	C
Probability of sale in 90 days	0.7	0.8	0.6

For every two cars of B, he should buy one car of type A or C. If he has Rs. 100,000 to invest what would he buy to maximize his expected gain? Formulate the above data into LPP.

20. An oil company has 2 units A and B which produce 3 different grades of oil; superfine, medium and low grade oil. The company has to supply 12, 8, 24 barrels of superfine, medium and low grade oils respectively per week. It costs the company Rs. 100 and Rs. 80 per day to run the units A and B respectively. Unit a produces 6, 2 and 4 barrels and unit B produces 2, 2 and 12 barrels of superfine, medium and low grade oil per day. The manager has to decide on how many days per week should each unit be operated in order to meet the requirement at minimum cost? Formulate the LPP and solve it graphically.

21. A company manufactures two types of school bags—a standard one and a deluxe model. Each bag requires four different operations, the details of which are listed below:

Department	Production time (in hours)		Availables Time (in hours)
	Standard	Deluxe	
Cutting and deying	1/10	1	630
Sewing	1/2	5/6	600
Finishing	1	2/3	708
Packaging	1/10	1/4	135

Each standard bag gives a profit of Rs. 10/- and deluxe bag Rs. 9/-. Formulate the LPP and solve graphically for maximizing the profit.

22. A company has two bottling plants, one at place X and the other at place Y. Each plant produce three types of drinks A, B and C. Plant located at place X can produces 1500, 3000 and 2000 bottles of A, B and C respectively per day. Plant located at place Y can produce 1500, 1000 and 5000 bottles of A, B, and C respectively per day. A market survey reveals that during the next month there will be a demand of 20,000 bottles of A, 30,000 bottles of B and 40,000 bottles of C. The operating cost/day of the plant located at place X is Rs. 600/- per day and that for the plant located at place Y is Rs. 400/- per day. For how many days each plant should be run during the next month so as to minimize the production cost at the same time meeting the market demand? Formulate the problem as a linear programming problem and solve the same by graphical method.

23. A manufacturer has five precision lathes, each with available 80 hours per week. He manufactures three different products on these lathes. Each unit of the product 1 takes 2 hours to machine, requires 1 kg of copper and 2 kg of steel and sells for Rs. 150/-. Each unit of product 3 takes 1 hour to machine, requires 2 kg of copper and 3 kg of steel and sells for Rs. 100/-. Each unit of product 3 requires Rs. 140/-. An adequate quantity of copper is available, but weekly quantity of steel available is 1000 kg. Contract commitments require that at least 100 units of product 1 be produced every week. The sales department estimates that more than 400 units of product 3 be sold every week. Copper costs Rs. 6/- per kg and steel costs Rs. 15/- per kg. The cost of machining is Rs. 150/- per hour. Formulate a LPP model to determine the optimal product mix. Do not solve.

24. PQR company makes two kinds of leather belts. Belt A is of high quality and belt B is of inferior quality. The profit margin for belt A is Re. 0.40/belt and for belt B is Re. 0.30/belt. Each belt of type A requires twice as much time as of belt B to manufacture. If all belts were of type B the company could make 1000 belts/day. The supply of leather is sufficient to make only 800 belts/day (both A and B combined). Belt A requires a fancy buckle and only 300/day are available. There are only 650 buckles/day available for belt B. Set up the LP equation and solve the problem graphically.

(May/June 1986)

25. A farmer has a 100-acre farm. He can sell all the tomatoes, lettuce or radishes he can raise. The price he can get is Re. 1 per kg. for tomatoes, Re. 0.75 a head for lettuce and Re. 2 per kg for radishes. The average yield per acre is 2000 kg of tomatoes, 3000 heads of lettuce and 1000 kg of radishes. Fertilizer is available at Re. 0.50 per kg and the amount required per acre is 100 kg each for tomatoes and lettuce and 50 kg for radishes. Labor required for sowing, cultivating and harvesting per acre is 5 man-days for tomatoes and radishes and 6 man-days for lettuce. A total of 400 man-days of labor are available at Rs. 20 per man-day. Formulate this problem as a LPP model to maximize the farmer's total profit. *(Sept./Oct. 1987)*

26. A customer of a chemical manufacturing unit needs 200 kg of a certain chemical consisting of two raw materials given below with their costs:

- Phosphate compound Rs. 14 per kg.
- Chromate compound Rs. 21 per kg.

The consumer's specification of the chemical product is as follows:

- The mix must contain at least 65 kg of chromate compound.
- The mix cannot contain more than 85 kg of phosphate compound.

Determine the least cost mix for a batch of 220 kg. *(Feb. 1988)*

27. A mining company owns two different mines that produce a given kind of ore in grades A, B and C. The mining company has contracted to provide smelting plant 12 tonnes of A, 8 tonnes of B and 24 tonnes of C grade ores per week. It costs the company Rs. 2000 per day to run the first mine and Rs. 1600 per day to run the second. In a day's operation, the first mine produces 6 tonnes of A, 2 tonnes of B and 4 tonnes of C grade ore, whereas the other mine produces daily 2 tonnes of A and 2 tonnes of C grade ores.

Formulate this problem as a LPP to determine how many days in a week each mine has to be operated to fulfil the company's orders most economically. *(July 1988)*

28. A farmer has to plant trees of two kinds A and B in a land 4,400 m^2 and B tree at least 40 m^2 of land. The annual water requirement of A is 30 units and B is 15 units per tree, while at most 3,300 units of water are available. It is also estimated that the ratio of the number of B trees to the number of A trees should not be less than 6/19 and should not be more than 17/8. The return per tree from A trees is expected to be 1.5 times as much as B tree. What should be the number of trees of each type to be planted, so that the expected return is maximum? *(March 1989)*

29. A firm manufactures two items A and B. It purchases castings which are then machined, bored and polished. Castings for items A and B cost Rs. 3 and Rs. 4 respectively and are sold at Rs. 6 and Rs. 7 each respectively. Running costs of the three machines are Rs. 20, Rs. 14 and Rs. 17.50 per hour respectively. What product mix maximizes the profit/capacities of the machines are: *(January 1990)*

	Part A	Part B
Machining capacity	25/hr	40/hr
Boring Capacity	28/hr	35/hr
Polishing Capacity	35/hr	25/hr

30. The company makes two kinds of belts A and B. Each belt of type A requires twice as much labor time as does each belt of type B. If all belts are type B, the company can produce a total of 500 belts/day. Type A requires a fancy buckle availability of which is limited to 200/day. The market limits daily sales of 150 and 200 of type A and type B respectively. The profit/belt of type A if Rs. 10/- and for type B is Rs. 8/-. Set up the LP equation and solve the problem graphically. *(Model Question Paper Aug. 1995)*

31. A company manufactures table fans and ceiling fans. The major manufacturing sections and their monthly production capacities are as follows:

Section	Table fan	Ceiling fan
Motor body and blades	800 or	10000 or suitable combinations
Winding and regulator	7000 or	12000 or suitable combinations
Table fan assembly	9000	
Ceiling fan assembly	10000	

The profit margin is Rs. 50/- per table fan and Rs. 30/- per ceiling fan. Determine the optimum product mix and corresponding profit.

(Model Question Paper Aug. 1995)

32. A firm produces P and Q which serve as fodder for cattle. These contain different amounts of nutritive ingredients N_1 and N_2 which are to be provided to the cattle in certain specified quantity. The products also contain an ingredient N_3 which is harmful if present in excessive quantities in the fodder. The following table gives the necessary data.

Ingredient	Amount present in the product		Minimum of maximum amount needed
	P	Q	
N_1	9	3	45 min
N_2	1	4	16 min
N_3	2	2	20 max

If the prices of P and Q per unit Rs. 20 and Rs. 40 respectively find the optimum product mix of the fodder with prescribed nutrient content. Use graphical method. *(Feb. 1996)*

33. A company makes cameras and binoculars on facilities F_1, F_2, F_3, F_4, F_5 and F_6 having production capacities as follows:

(Aug. 1996)

Facility	Production capacity
F_1	100 Cameras or 150 binoculars
F_2	80 Cameras or 150 binoculars
F_3	100 Cameras or 200 binoculars
F_4	120 Cameras or 90 binoculars
F_5 (testing shop)	60 Cameras
F_6 (testing shop)	60 Binoculars

Facility F_1 to F_4 can be planned for sharing the production of cameras and binoculars. F_5 and F_6 are respective testing facilities for testing cameras and binoculars separately. If the profit contributions of cameras and binoculars are Rs. 40/- and 30/- respectively. Determine the product mix for maximum profit.

34. A manufacturer produces two types of models M_1 and M_2. Each M_1 model requires 4 hours of grinding and 2 hours of polishing, whereas each M_2 model requires 2 hours of grinding and 5 hours of polishing. The manufacturer has 2 grinders and 3 polishers. Each grinder has 40 hours a week and each polisher works 60 hours a week. Profit on M_1 model is Rs. 3 and on M_2 model is Rs. 4. Whatever is produced in a week is sold in the market, how should the manufacturer allocate his production capacity to the two types of models so that he may make the maximum profit in a week?

(Feb. 1996)

35. Old hens can be bought at Rs. 20 each and young ones at Rs. 50 each. The old hens lay 3 eggs/week and the young ones lay 5 eggs/week, each egg being worth Rs. 3/-. It costs Rs. 10 per week to feed a hen. If there are only Rs. 800 available to be spent on purchasing the hens. How many of each kind of hens should be bought in order to have a maximum profit per week assuming that it is not possible to house more than 20 hens at a time?

(Aug. 2001)

36. A company has two grades of inspectors A and B. It is required that at least 1800 pieces be inspected per day in 8 hours. Grade A inspectors can check at the rate of 25 pieces/hour with an accuracy of 98%. Grade B inspectors check at the rate of 15 pieces/

hour with 96% accuracy. The wage rate for grade A inspectors is Rs. 20/hr and that of grade B Rs. 15/hr. Each time an error is made by any inspector the cost to the company is Rs. 10/-. There are 8 grade A inspectors and 10 grade B inspectors available for service. Determine the optimum assignment of inspectors that will minimize the total cost of inspection. Solve graphically.

(Feb. 1997)

37. A company manufacturers radios and calculators. The radios contribute Rs. 10 per unit and the calculators Rs. 15 per unit to profits. Each radio requires 4 diodes and 4 resistors while each calculator requires 10 diodes and 2 resistors. The radios take 12 min. and calculators take 9.6 min. of time on the company's electronic testing machine and the product manager estimates that 16 hours of test time are available. The firm has 8000 diodes and 3000 resistors in inventory. What mix of products should be selected to get maximum profit?

(March/April 2000)

38. A company produces two types of hats. Each hat of the first type requires twice as much labor time as does each hat of the second type. If all the hats produced are of second type, then company can produce 500 hats a day. The market limit daily sales of the first and second types to 150 and 200 hats respectively. Assume that the profit per hat is Rs. 12 for type 1 and Rs. 8/- for the type 2. Determine the number of hats of each type to produce to maximize the profit.

(Aug. 1997)

39. A company manufacturing medicines proposes to produce two medicines A and B. There are sufficient ingredients available to produce 10000 bottles of A and 20000 bottles of B. There are only 23,000 bottles available into which either of the medicines can be filled. It takes three hours to produce 1000 bottles of A and one hour to produce 1000 bottles of B and 33 production hours available for the operation. The company earns a profit of Rs. 16 per bottle of A and Rs. 14 per bottle of B. Determine the optimum product mix using graphical method.

40. A company producing three different products use two types of raw materials A and B of which 200 and 300 units are available. Raw material requirements are given below:

Raw material	Requirements for		
	Product I	Product II	Product III
A	2	3	5
B	4	2	7

Labor requirement of product I is twice that of product II and three times that of product III. The maximum number of product II that can be produced is 70 units. The profit per unit of products I, II and III are Rs. 30, Rs. 20 and Rs. 50 respectively. *(Sept./Oct. 1998)*

41. The manufacturer of a patent medicine proposes to prepare a production plan for medicines A and B. There are sufficient ingredients available to make 20,000 bottles of medicine A and 40,000 bottles of medicine B, but there are only 45,000 bottles into which either of the medicines can be filled. Further it takes 3 hours to prepare enough material to fill 1000 bottles of medicine A and 1 hour to prepare enough material to fill 1000 bottles of medicine B and there are 66 hours available for this operation. The profit is Rs. 8 per bottle for medicine A and Rs. 7 per bottle for medicine B. Determine optimum product mix. *(March/April1998)*

42. A manufacturer makes two products A and B each of which is processed through four departments 1, 2, 3 and 4 in some order. Product A could be manufactured either by passing it through departments 1-3-4 or 2-3-4, product B needs processing through departments 2-3-4 only. Their rates of processing in the departments and profits per unit product are given as under: *(Aug. 1995)*

Product	Profit Rs/unit	Rates of process units/week departments			
		1	2	3	4
A	500	5	—	5	10
A	450	—	4	5	5
B	550	—	2	5	8

The company works on 50 week year basis but down time in the department varies and expected number of production weeks from departments 1, 2, 3 and 4 are 45, 42, 48 and 45 respectively. There is a sales commitment of 50 units of product A and 50 units of product B every year. Find the optimal solution.

43. Consider the following problem faced by a production planner in a soft drink plant. He has two bottling machines A and B. A is designed for 8 ounce bottles and B for 16 ounce bottles. However, each can be used on both types with some loss of efficiency. The following data is available.

Machine	8 ounce bottles	16 ounce bottles
A	100/min	50/min
B	60/min	89/min

The machines can be run 8 hours/day. Profit on an 8 ounce bottle is Rs. 1.50 and on 16 ounce bottle is Rs. 2.50. Weekly production of the bottles cannot exceed 300,000 ounces and the market can absorb only 25,000, 8 ounce bottles and 7000, 16 ounce bottles/week. The planner wishes to maximize his profit. Formulate and solve.

44. The village butcher shop traditionally makes its meat from a combination of lean ground beef and ground pork. The ground beef contains 80% meat and 20% fat and costs the shop Rs. 80 per kg. The ground pork contains 68% meat and 32% fat and costs Rs. 60 per kg. How much of each kind of meat should the shop use in each kg of meat loaf if it wants to minimize its cost and to keep the fat content of the meat loaf to not more than 25% solve graphically. *(Aug. 1995)*

45. A factory is engaged in manufacturing three products A, B and C which involve lathe work, grinding and assembly. The cutting, grinding and assembly times required for one unit of A are 2, 1 and 1 hours respectively. Similarly, they are 3, 1 and 3 hours for one unit of B and 1, 2 and 1 hours for one unit of C. The profits on A, B and C are Rs. 4, 3 and 5 per unit respectively. Assuming that there are 300 hrs of lathe time, 300 hrs of grinding time and 240 hrs of assembly time, how may units of each product should be produced in order to maximize profit? *(Aug. 1995)*

46. A carpenter purchased 100 sq. meters of plywood scrap and 9 meters of some mica at a very cheap rate for manufacturing a dining table and a showcase. A dining table requires 12 sq. meters of plywood and 16 sq. meters sunmica and a showcase requires 16 sq. meters of plywood and 8 sq. meters of sunmica. He earns a profit of Rs. 40/-

and 50/- per dining table and showcase. What would be the mix for max profit?

47. An electric furnace is used to melt iron to make grey iron castings and charge of 2 tonnes is required. The product must meet the following material specifications:

- Carbon percentage 3.25 (min) and 3.40 (max).
- Silicon percentage 2.05 (min) and 2.25 (max).

The materials available to make this product are:

Material	Carbon %	Silicon %	Cost in Rs.
Steel scrap A	0.45	0.10	600/tonne
Steel scarp B	0.40	0.15	630/tonne
Cast Iron scarp	3.50	2.30	680/tonne
Foundry remelt	100.00	2.20	400/tonne
Carbon briquettes	100.00	0	3/kg
Silicon briquettes	0	100.00	5/kg

Formulate a LP problem with an appropriate objective and constraints.

48. An organization is interested in producing two varieties of PCB's for the ensuring production schedule. PCB type A is required in minimum quantity of 50 whereas PCB type B is required in minimum quantity of 35. Due to maintenance considerations the number of PCB's of type B be at least 10. The production process involves assembly on a robot controlled assembler and soldering by wave soldering m/c. Every PCB of type A will cost Rs. 1400/-. Every PCB of type A costs 800/- for processing on wave soldering m/c and the type B costs Rs. 1000/-. Find how the company should plan its production cost. Formulate this as an LPP and solve the same by using BIG M simplex procedure.

49. A home decorator manufactures 2 types of lamps say A and B. Both the lamps go through 2 technicians, first a cutter and second a finisher. Lamp A requires 2 hrs of cutter's time and 1 hr's of finisher's time. Lamp B requires 1 hr of cutter's time and 2 hrs of finisher's time. The cutter has 104 hrs and finisher has 76 hrs of time available time each month. Profit on one lamp A is Rs. 6/- and on B is Rs. 11/-. Assume that he can sell that he produces. Formulate the above problem as LPP and solve it. **Answer 440**

50. A firm uses lathe machines, milling machines and grinding machines to produce two machine parts. Table below gives the machining times require. For each part, the machining time available for different machines and profit on each machine part.

Types of machines	Time required (mins)		Max. time available
	Part 1	Part 2	
Lathe	12	16	3000
Milling	4	10	2000
Grinding	2	3	9000
Profit	Rs. 40/-	Rs. 100/-	

Answer 20,000

51. A company sells two different products A and B. The company makes a profit of Rs. 40/- and Rs. 30/- per unit on product A and B respectively. The two products are produced in a common production process and are sold in two different markets. The production has a capacity of 30000 man/hrs. It takes 3 hrs to produce one unit of B. The market has been surveyed and company officials feel that the maximum number of units of A that can be sold is 8000 and maximum of B is 12. Formulate the problem as LPP and solve it. **Answer 6,00,000**

52. A firm can produce 3 types of cloth A, B and C. Three kinds of wool are required for it, say red, green and blue wool. One unit length of type A cloth needs 3 yards of red wool, 3 yards of blue wool. One unit length of type B needs 3 yards of red, 2 yards of green and 2 yards of blue wool. Type C needs 5 yards of green and 4 yards of blue. The firm has only a stock of 8 yards of red, 10 yards of green and 15 yards of blue. It is assumed that the income obtained from 1 unit of length of type A is Rs. 3/-, type B is Rs. 5/- and type C is Rs. 4/-. Formulate and solve.

53. Two grades of paper M and N are produced on a paper machine because of raw material restriction not more that 400 tonnes of grade 'M' and 300 tonnes of grade 'M' can be provided in a week. There are 160 hrs production in a week. It requires 0.2, 0.4 hr to produce one tonne of products 'M' and 'N' respectively, with the corresponding profits of Rs. 20/- and Rs. 50/- per tonne. Formulate and solve. **Answer 19,000**

54. Consider two different types of food say f_1 and f_2. Assume that these foods contain v_1, v_2 and v_3 vitamins respectively. Minimum daily requirement of these vitamins are 1 mg of v_1, 50 mg of v_2 and 10 mg of v_3. Suppose that the food f_1 contains 1 mg of v_1, 100 mg of v_2 cost of 1 unit of f_1 if Rs. 1/- and cost of f_2 is Rs. 1.50/-. Formulate and solve. **Answer 1**

55. A warehouse company has Rs. 1.5 million for allocation of its warehouse. Three productions A, B and C repuire 30, 3, 15 m^2 of space per unit respectively and 3 lack m^2 of space is available. Production cost A Rs. 12/-, product B cost Rs. 4.5/- and C cost Rs. 15/-. The sale prices of A, B and C are Rs. 15/-, Rs. 6/- and Rs. 12/- respectively, formulate the above problem as LPP and solve it.

56. The maximum amounts available for crude A and B are 200 units and 150 units respectively, the market requirement shows that at least 100 units of gasoline X and 80 units of gasoline Y must be produced. The profit for production run for process 1 and process 2 are Rs. 300/- and Rs. 400/- respectively. Formulate and solve.

Answer 13,848

57. A company has 2 bottling plants one located at Bangalore and other at Mysore. Each plant produces 3 brands of drink A, B and C. Bangalore can produce in a day 1500, 3000 and 2000 bottles of A, B and C respectively while the capacity of Mysore plant is 1500, 1000 and 5000 bottles of A, B and C respectively. Market survey indicates that during the month of April there will a demand of 20,000 bottles of A, 40,000 bottles of B and 44,000 bottles of C. The operating cost per day for the plant at Bangalore is Rs. 6000/-, while the operating cost of Mysore plant is Rs. 400/-. For how many days each plant should be run in April, so as to minimize the production cost while still meeting the market demand. Formulate and solve.

Answer 8,800

58. The postmaster of a local post office wishes to have extra helpers during Diwali season because of large increase in the volume of mails handling and delivery. Because of limited office space the number of temporary helpers should not exceed 10. According to the past experience men can handle 300 letters and 80 packages per day and women can handle 100 letters and 60 packages per day. The postman believes that daily volume of extra letters and packages will not be less than 3,400 and 680 respectively. A man receives Rs. 25/- a day. Formulate the above problem in order to determine the number of men and women helpers to be hired to keep the pay role at a minimum.

59. A company manufactures washing machine and the dryers. The major manufacturing department and their monthly capacities are as follows:

Department	Monthly capacity	
	Washer	Dryer
Stamping	10,000	10,000
Motor and transmission	16,000	7000
Assembly time for washer	9000	
Assembly time for dryer		5000

The contribution to profit is Rs. 900/- per washer and Rs. 1000/- per dryer. Determine the optimum product mix and the corresponding profit. **Answer 94,66,660**

60. A manufacturer makes straight chairs and rotating chairs. For each type of chair he uses major production areas of cutting, dipping and assembly. The capacities of three departments are given below:

- Cutting: 400 straight or 300 rotating or any combination.
- Dipping: 400 straight or 400 rotating or any combination.
- Assembly: 250 straight or 200 rotation or any combination.

From straight chair he makes a profit of Rs. 10/- and from rotating chair he makes Rs. 20/-. Determine optimum. Product mix and the corresponding profit. **Answer 4,000**

61. ABC company owns a paint factory that produces both exterior and interior paints for the wholesale distribution. Two basic raw materials A and B are used to manufacture the paints. The maximum availability of A is 6 tonnes per day and that of B is 8 tonnes per day. The daily requirements of raw material per tonne of interior and exterior are given below:

Raw material	Exterior	Interior	Max. availabity
A	1	2	6
B	2	1	8

Market survey has established that the daily demand for interior paint cannot exceed that of exterior paint by more that 1 tonne. The survey also shows that maximum demand for interior paint is limited to two tonnes per day. The wholesale price per tonne is Rs. 3000/- for interior paint. How interior and exterior paints the company should produce to maximize the gross income? Formula and solve.

Answer 12,650

62. A student has two final exams to prepare for. Each hour of study he devotes to OR is expected a return of Rs. 6000/- in items of large benefit. Each hour devoted on SQC; is a expected a return of Rs. 300/- in terms of long range benefit. All shops are closed and the student has only 15 cigarettes, he feels that he needs 1 cigarette every 20 minutes while studying SQC and 1 every 12 minutes while studying OR. Time is running short and only 4 hrs remain to prepare for exams. It is necessary that the student would like to maximize his returns and for the effort he puts. Formulate this problem as LPP and solve it. **Answer 1,800**

63. An aviation fuel manufacturer sells two types of fuel. Type A fuel is 255 grade 1 gasoline, 255 grade 2 gasoline and 505 of grade 3 gasoline. Type B fuel is 50% grade 2 and 50% of grade 3 gasoline. Available for production are 500 liter per hour of grade 1 and 200 liter of grade 2 and 3. Costs are Rs. 3/- per liter of grade 1 and Rs. 6/- per liter of grade 2 and Rs. 5/- per liter of grade 3. Type A can be sold for Rs. 60/- per liter and type B for Rs. 80/- per liter. How much of each fuel should be made? If we can increase the price of type A fuel, at what price should we sell type A fuel to increase his profit by 20%.

64. A trucking company with Rs. 4000,000/- to spent on new equipment is contemplating three types of vehicles. Vehicle A has 10 tonnes pay load and is expected to average 35 km per hour and cost Rs. 30,000/-. Vehicle B has a 20 tonnes pay load and expected to average 30 km per hour and cost Rs. 110,000/-. Vehicle C is a modified form of B has sleeping quarters for one driver. This reduces its capacity by 18 tonnes and rises its cost by Rs. 15,000/-. Vehicle A requires a crew and of one man and if driver on 3 shifts per day could be run from average of 18 hrs/day. Vehicle B and C require a crew of two men each but whereas B would be driven 18 hrs/day. The company has 150 drivers available each day. The maintenance facilities are such that the total number of vehicle should not exceed 30, formulate this as LPP and set up the equation under the list simplex table maximizes for km.

65. A company can advertise its product using radio and TV station. In budget limit the advertisement cannot exceed Rs. 10000 per month. Each minute of radio advertisement costs Rs. 50/- and each minute of TV advertisement costs Rs. 1000/-. The company would like to use radio at least twice as much as TV. The past experience shows that each minute of TV generates 25 times of radio advertisement. Determine the optimum allocation of monthly budget to radio and TV advertisements using graphical method.

66. A furniture maker has 6 units of wood and 28 hrs of free time, in which he will make decorative screens. Two models have sold well in the past. So he will restrict himself to those two. Model I, requires 2 units of wood and 7 hrs time while model II requires 1 unit of wood and 8 hrs of time. The prices of the models are Rs. 1200 and Rs. 800 respectively. Formulate this as an LPP and optimize the sales revenue of the furniture maker.

67. An oil refinery wishes to blend four petroleum constituents to make of petrol A, B and C. The availability of the constituents and costs are given below:

Constituent	Quantity available in barrels per day	Cost per barrel rupees
1	3,500	3,000
2	2,000	6,000
3	3,000	4,000
4	1,500	5,000

To maintain the required quantity of each grade petrol the following specifications are given along with the selling price for each grade.

Grade	Specifications	Selling price Rs/barrel
A	Not more than 30% of 1 Not less than 40% of 2 Not more than 50% of 3	5,000
B	Not more than 50% of 1 Not less than 10% of 2	4,500
C	Not more than 70% of 1	3,500

Set up a linear programming model for determining the amount of blend in each grade of petrol to maximize the profit.

68. An animal feed manufacturer has to produce 200 kg of feed mixture consisting of two ingredients A and B. A costs Rs. 6/- kg and B costs Rs. 16/- kg. Not more than 80 kg of A can be used and at least 60 kg of B must be used. Using simplex method find the optimum product mix.

69. A firm produces three products. These products are processed on three different machines. The time required to manufacture one unit of each of the three products are the daily capacity of the 3 machines if given in the table below:

Machine	Time in units			Machine capacity
	1	2	3	
M1	2	3	2	440
M2	4	—	3	470
M3	2	5	—	430

It is assumed that all the products produced are consumed in the market. The profit per unit for products 1, 2 and 3 are Rs. 4/-, Rs. 3/-, and Rs. 6/- respectively. Formulate a LP model and find the number of units of each product manufactured.

70. A company manufactures two products A and B. These products are processed on the same machine. It takes 10 minutes to process one unit of A and 2 minutes for each unit of product B. Machine operates for a maximum of 35 hours in a week. Product A requires 1 kg of raw material per unit while B requires 0.5 kg per unit. The supply of raw material is limited to 600 kg per week. Market constraint on product B is known to be 800 units per week. If product

A costs Rs. 5/- per unit and can be sold at Rs. 10/- per unit and product B costs Rs. 6/- per unit but can be sold at a unit price of Rs. 8/-, determine how many units of product A and B should be produced in order to maximize the profit.

71. A manufacturer of leather belts makes 3 types of belts A, B and C, which are processed on 3 machines M_1, M_2 and M_3. Belt A requires 2 hours on machine M_1 and 3 hours on machine M_3. Belt B requires 3 hours on machine M_1, 2 hours on machine M_2 and 2 hours on machine M_3. Belt C requires 5 hours on machine M_2 and 4 hours on machine M_3. There are 8 hours of time per day on machine M_1, 10 hours per day on machine M_2 and 15 hours per day on machine M_3. The profit gained from belt A is Rs. 3 per unit, from belt B is Rs. 5 per unit and from C Rs. 4 per unit. What should be the daily production of each type of belts so that the profit is maximum?

72. A manufacturer of furniture makes two products—tables and chairs. Processing of these products is done on two machines A and B. A chair requires 5 hours on machine A and 8 hours on machine B. A table requires 6 hours on machine A and 2 hours on machine B. There are 30 hours of time per day available on machine A and 12 hours available on machine B. Profit gained by the manufacturer from a chair is Re. 1 and that from a table is Rs. 5.

- Formulate the problem for maximizing profits.
- Write the dual of the above problem.
- Solve the dual by graphical method.

73. An organization is interested in producing two varieties of PCB's for ensuring production schedule. PCB type A is required in minimum quantity of 50 whereas PCB type B is required in minimum quantity of 35. Due to maintenance considerations the number of PCB's of type B by a least 10. The production process involves assembly on a robot controlled assembler and soldering by wave soldering machine. Every PCB of type A will cost Rs. 2000 for processing on the assembler and Rs. 800 for processing on the wave soldering machine. Every PCB of type B will cost Rs. 1400 for processing on the robot assembler and Rs. 1000 for processing on the wave soldering machine. Find how the company should plan its production so as to minimize the production cost.

74. A company wishes to plan its advertising strategy for a new computer product. Two magazines are under consideration and one is a weekly and the other is a monthly. The weekly has 2000 potential customers whereas the monthly has 3000 in one page of advertising. The cost of advertising per page in the weekly and monthly is Rs. 400 and Rs. 600 respectively. The company has a budget of Rs. 6,000 per month for the advertisement. There is an important requirement that the total reach for the income group under Rs. 20,000 per annum should not exceed 4000 potential customers. The reach of the weekly and the monthly for this income group is 400 and 200 potential customers per page respectively. How many pages should be bought in the two magazines to maximize reach subject to this condition? **Answer 30,000**

2

Graphically and Simplex Problems

1. Solve the following LPP by graphical method. Draw ZZ lines, one of which must pass through optimal solution:

Maximize $Z=5X_1+4X_2$

STC

$6X_1+4X_2<=24$

$X_1+2X_2 <=1200$

$-X_1+X_2 <=1$

$X_2 <=1$

$X_1, X_2, >=0$

2. Solve the following LPP graphically;

Minimize $Z = 7x_1 + 3x_2$

Subject to $X_1 + 2x_2 > = 3$

$X_1 + X_2 < = 4$

$X_1 < = 5/2$

$X_2 < = 3/2$

$X_1, X_2 > = 0$

3. Solve the following LPP

Minimum $Z = 2x_1 - 3x_2 + 4x_3$

Subject to $X_1 + x_2 - 2x_3 > = 12$

$X_1 + 4x_3 < = 20$

$3x_2 - X_3 = 15$

$X_1, X_2, X_3 > = 0$

4. A company makes three products X, Y and Z out of three raw materials A, B and C. The number of units of raw materials required to produce one unit of product is as given below.

		Product		
		X	**Y**	**Z**
Raw	A	1	2	1
Material	B	2	1	4
	C	2	5	1

The unit profit contribution of products X, Y and Z are Rs. 40, Rs. 25 and Rs. 50 respectively. The number of raw material units available are 36, 60 and 45 respectively. Determine, through simplex method, the product mix that will maximize the total profit. Write the solution simplex to the dual problem and give the economic interpretation.

5. Solve the following LPP either by Big-M method by dual simplex method.

Minimize $Z = 2x_1 + X_2$

Such that

$$X_1 + X_2 >= 4$$

$$2x_1 - X_2 >= 3$$

$$X_1, X_2 >= 0$$

6. Solve using simplex method

$$Z = 40x_1 + 30x_2$$

Subject to

$$2x_1 + x_2 <= 1000$$

$$x_1 + x_2 <= 800$$

$$x_1 <= 400$$

$$x_2 <= 700$$

$$x_1 >= 0 \quad x_2 >= 0$$

7. Solve the following LPP using Big-M method.

Minimize $Z = 2x_1 + 5x_2$

Subject to : $X_1 + X_2 = 100$

$X_1 <= 40$

$X_2 >= 30$

$X_1, X_2 >= 0$

8. Write the dual of the following:

Minimize $Z = X_1 - 3x_2 - 2x_3$

STC $3x_1 - X_2 + 2x_3 <= 7$

$2x_1 - 4x_2 >= 12$

$-4x_1 + 3x_2 + 8x_3 = 10$

$X_1, X_2 >= 0$, X_3 is unrestricted.

9. Solve the following LPP by Big-M technique

Maximize $= 3X_1 + 2X_2 + X_3$

STC

$-3X_1 + 3X_2 + 2X_3 = 8$

$-3X_1 + 3X_2 + X_3 = 7$

$X_1, X_2, X_3, >= 0$

10. Solve the following linear programming problem by using simplex method:

Minimize $Z = 4X_1 + 2X_2$

STC

$3X_1 + X_2 >= 27$

$-X_1 - X_2 <= -21$

$X_1 + 2X_2 >= 30$

$X_1, X_2, >= 0$

11. Solve the following LPP using simplex method:

Maximize $Z = 5X_1+6 X_2$

STC

$2X_1+5 X_2 <=1500$

$3X_1+X_2 <=1200$

$X_1, X_2, >=0$

12. Solve the following LPP graphically:

Minimize $Z = 5X_1+3X_2$

STC

$3X_1+5X_2 <=15$

$5X_1+2X_2 <=10$

$X_1, X_2, >=0$

13. Solve the following LPP graphically

Maximize $Z=2X_1+X_2$

STC

$X_2 <=10$

$2X_1+X_2 <=60$

$X_1+X_2 <=18$

$3X_1+X_2 <=44$

$X_1, X_2, >=0$

14. Solve the following LPP:

Maximum $Z=3X_1+2 X_2+X_3$

STC

$-3X_1+2X_2+8X_3=8$

$-3X_1+4X_2+8X_3=7$

$X_1, X_2, X_3 >=0$

15. Solve the following LPP by graphical method.

Maximum $Z=3X_1+5X_2$

STC

$4X_1+6X_2 >=10$

$2X_1+3X_2 <= 30$

$-X_1+X_2 <=4$

$X_1-2X_2 >=12$

$X_1, X_2, >=0$

16. Solve the following LPP

Minimize $Z = Z=4X_1+2X_2$

STC

$3X_1+2X_2 >=27$

$-X_1-2X_2 <= -21$

$X_1+2X_2 >=30$

$X_1, X_2 >=0$

17. Solve the following LPP

Minimize $Z =2X_1+2X_2+4X_3$

STC

$2X_1+3X_2+5X_3 <=3$

$3X_1+2X_2+7X_3 <= 5$

$X_1,$ X2, X3 >=0

18. Solve the following LPP

Minimize $Z=6X_1-5X_2+4X_3$

STC

$2X_1+X_2-6X_3=20$

$6X_1+5X_2+10X_3 <= 76$

$-8X_1+3X_2-6X_3 >= -50$

$X_1, X_2, X_3 >=0$

19. Solve the simplex method:

Maximum $Z=X_1+2X_2+3X_3+3X_4$

STC

$X_1+2X_2+X_3+X_4 <=10$

$X_1+2X_2+3X_3 = 15$

$2X_1+X_2+5X_3 >= 20$

$X_1, X_2, X_3, X_4 >=0$

20. Solve the following LPP

Maximum $Z=2X_1+5X_2$

STC

$2X_2 <=8$

$3X_1 <= 4$

$0 <= 2X_2 <=3$

X_1 is unrestricted.

21. Solve the following LPP by using Big-M method.

Maximum $Z=3X_1+2X_2+X_3$

STC

$-3X_1+2X_2+2X_3 =8$

$-3X_1+4X_2+X_3 = 7$

$X_1, X_2, X_3 >=0$

22. Solve the following LPP by simplex method:

Minimize $Z = 2X_1+X_2$

STC

$3X_1+X_2 =3$

$4X_1+3X_2 >=6$

$X_1+2X_2 <=3$

$X_1, X_2, >=0$

23. Solve the following LPP graphically

Maximum $Z = 100X_1+50X_2$

STC

$4X_1+6X_2 <=24$

$X_1 <=4$

$X_2 <=4/3$

$X_1, X_2, >=0$

24. Solve the following LPP by simplex method.

Maximum $Z = 5X_1+2X_2+10X_3$

STC

$X_1 - X_3 <= 10$

$X_2 - 3X_3 >= 10$

$X_1 + X_2 + X_3 <= 10$

$X_{1,} X_{2,} X_3 >=0$

25. Consider the following LP problem

Minimize $Z = 100X_1+200X_2+150X_3$

STC

$5X_1+20X_2+30X_3 <=60$

$10X_1+20X_2+50X_3 <= 100$

$X_{1,} X_2 X_3 >=0$

26. Solve the following LPP

Maximum $Z = X_1+2X_2+3X_3$

STC

$X_1+2X_2+3X_3 =15$

$2X_1+X_2+5X_3 = 20$

$X_1+2X_2+X_3 <= 8$

$X_{1,} X_2 X_3 >=0$

27. Maximum $Z = 2x_1 + x_2$

Subject to the constraints:

$$X_1 + 2x_2 < 10$$
$$X_1 + x_2 < 6$$
$$X_1 - x_2 < 2$$
$$X_1 - 2x_2 < 1$$

and $x_1, x_2 > 0$. Solve graphically.

28. Solve graphically or otherwise the following LPP:

Maximum $Z = 8x_1 + 3x_2$

Such that :

$$x_1 + 2x_2 < 20$$
$$2x_1 + x_2 < 20$$
$$x_1 + x_2 < 12$$
$$x_i > 0 \text{ for all } i$$

3

Big M Method Problems

1. Solve the following LPP by big M technique

Maximize $= 3X_1+2X_2+X_3$

STC

$-3X_1+2X_2+2X_3=8$

$-3X_1+4X_2+X_3=7$

$X_1, X_2, X_3, >=0$

2. Solve the following linear programming problem by using simplex method:

Minimize $Z=4X_1+2X_2$

STC

$3X_1+X_2>=27$

$-X_1-X_2<=-21$

$X_1+2X_2>=30$

$X_1, X_2, >=0$

3. Solve the following LPP using simplex method:

Maximize $Z=5X_1+6X_2$

STC

$2X_1+5X_2<=1500$

$3X_1+X_2<=1200$

$X_1, X_2, >=0$

4. Solve the following LPP graphically:

Minimize $Z=5X_1+3X_2$

STC

$$3X_1+5X_2<=15$$
$$5X_1+2X_2<=10$$
$$X_1, X_2, >=0$$

5. Solve the following LPP graphically:

Maximize $Z=2X_1+X_2$

STC

$$X_2 <=10$$
$$2X_1+X_2<=60$$
$$X_1+X_2<=18$$
$$3X_1+X_2<=44$$
$$X_1, X_2, >=0$$

6. Solve the following LPP:

Maximum $Z=3X_1+2\ X_2+X_3$

STC

$$-3X_1+2X_2+2X_3=8$$
$$-3X_1+4X_2+X_3=7$$
$$X_1, X_2, X_3 >=0$$

7. Solve the following LPP by graphical method.

Maximum $Z=3X_1+5X_2$

STC

$$4X_1+6X_2 >=10$$
$$2X_1+3X_2<= 30$$
$$-X_1+X_2<=4$$
$$X_1-2X_2>=12$$
$$X_1, X_2, >=0$$

8. Solve the following LPP

Minimize $Z = Z=4X_1+2X_2$

STC

$3X_1+2X_2 >=27$

$-X_1-2X_2 <= -21$

$X_1+2X_2 >=30$

$X_{1,}X_2 >=0$

9. Solve the following LPP

Minimize $Z =2X_1+2X_2+4X_3$

STC

$2X_1+3X_2 +5X_3 <=3$

$3X_1+2X_2+7X_3 <= 5$

$X_{1,}$ X2, X3 >=0

10. Solve the following LPP

Minimize $Z=6X_1-5X_2+4X_3$

STC

$2X_1+X_2 -6X_3=20$

$6X_1+5X_2+10X_3 <= 76$

$-8X_1+3X_2 -6X_3>= -50$

$X_{1,}X_2 ,X_3 >=0$

11. Solve the simplex method:

Maximum $Z=X_1+2X_2+3X_3 +3X_4$

STC

$X_1+2X_2 +X_3+X_4 <=10$

$X_1+2X_2+3X_3 = 15$

$2X_1+X_2 +5X_3>= 20$

$X_{1,}X_{2,} X_{3,} X_4 >=0$

12. Solve the following LPP

Maximum $Z=2X_1+5X_2$

STC

$2X_2 <=8$

$3X_1 <= 4$

$0<= 2X_2<=3$

X_1 unrestricted

13. Solve the following LPP by using Big-M method.

Maximum $Z=3X_1+2X_2+X_3$

STC

$6X_1+2X_2+2X_3 =8$

$9X_1+4X_2+X_3= 7$

$X_{1,}X_{2,} X_3 >=0$

14. Solve the following LPP by simplex method:

Minimize $Z = 2X_1+X_2$

STC

$3X_1+X_2 =3$

$4X_1+3X_2>=6$

$X_1+2X_2<=3$

$X_1, X_2, >=0$

15. Solve the following LPP graphically

Maximum $Z = 100X_1+50X_2$

STC

$4X_1+6X_2 <=24$

$X_1<=4$

$X_2<=4/3$

$X_1, X_2, >=0$

16. Solve the following LPP by simplex method.

Maximum $Z=5X_1+2X_2+10X_3$

STC

$$X_1-X_3 <= 10$$
$$X_2-3X_3 >=10$$
$$X_1+X_2+X_3 <= 10$$
$$X_{1,}X_{2,}X_3 >=0$$

17. Consider the following LP problem

Minimize $Z = 100X_1+200X_2+150X_3$

STC

$$5X_1+20X_2+30X_3 <=60$$
$$10X_1+20X_2+50X_3 <= 100$$
$$X_{1,}X_2\ X_3>=0$$

18. Solve the following LPP

Maximum $Z = X_1+2X_2+3X_3$

STC

$$X_1+2X_2+3X_3 =15$$
$$2X_1+X_2+5X_3 = 20$$
$$X_1+2X_2+X_3 <= 8$$
$$X_{1,}X_2\ X_3>=0$$

19. Explain the various situations where the idea of operation research can be employed.

Solve the following using simplex method.

$$Z = 15x_1 + 6x_2 + 27x_3 + 8x_4$$

Subject to
$$9x_1 + 3x_2 + 21x_3 + 6x_4 < 450$$
$$15x_1 + 24x_3 + 12x_4 < 330$$
$$12x_1 + 24x_2 + 15x_3 + 9x_4 < 540$$

20. Use simplex method to solve the following:

Maximize $Z = 3x_1 + 5x_2 + 4x_3$

Subject to

$$2x_1 + 3x_2 < 8$$
$$3x_1 + 2x_2 + 4x_3 < 15$$
$$2x_2 + 5x_3 < 10$$
$$x_1, x_2, x_3 > 0.$$

21. Solve the given LPP:

$$Z_{max} = 4x_1 + x_2 + 3x_3 + 5x_4$$

Subject to the constraints:

$$4x_1 - 6x_2 - 5x_3 + 4x_4 > -20$$
$$3x_1 - 2x_2 + 4x_3 + x_4 < 10$$
$$8x_1 - 3x_2 + 3x_3 + 2x_4 < 20$$
$$x_1, x_2, x_3, x_4 > 0.$$

and show that it has an unbounded solution.

22. Solve the following LPP.

Maximum $Z = 2x_1 + 3x_2 + 4x_3$

STC
$$-x_1 - x_2 - x_3 > -1$$
$$x_1 + x_2 + 2x_3 = 2$$
$$3x_1 + 2x_2 + x_3 > 4$$
$x_1, x_2, > 0$, x_3 is unrestricted.

23. Using Big-M method solve the following LPP:

Maximize $Z = 3x_1 + 2x_2 + 3x_3$

Subject to the constraints:

$$2x_1 + x_2 + x_3 < 2$$
$$3x_1 + 4x_2 + 2x_3 > 8$$
$$x_1, x_2, x_3 > 0$$

24. Solve the following LPP.

Maximum $Z = 2x_1 + 3x_2 + 4x_3$

STC $-x_1 - x_2 - x_3 > -1$

$x_1 + x_2 + 2x_3 = 2$

$3x_1 + 2x_2 + x_3 > 4$

$x_1, x_2, > 0$, x_3 is unrestricted.

25. Solve the following LPP by simplex method and also give the optimal values of the dual variable of the given LPP.

Maximum $Z = 3X_1+2X_2$

STC

$-X_1+2X_2 <=4$

$3X_1+2X_2 <=14$

$X_1-X_2 <=3$

$X_1, X_2, >=0$

Does the problem have unique solution? If not, determine the alternate solution also.

26. Solve the following linear programming problem:

Maximum $Z = x_1 + 2x_2 + 3x_3 - x_4$

s.t.,

$x_1 + 2x_2 + 3x_3 = 15$

$2x_1 + x_2 + 5x_3 <= 20$

$X_1 + 2x_2 + x_3 + x_4 = 10$

$X_i > 0$ i=1,2,3,4

4

Duality and Dual Simplex Problems

1. Using the dual simplex method solve the following LPP

Minimize $Z=6X_1+7X_2+3X_3+5X_4$

STC

$$5X_1+6X_2-3X_3+4X_4>=12$$
$$X_2+5X_3-6X_4>=10$$
$$2X_1+5X_2+X_3+X_4>=8$$
$$X_1, X_2, X_3, X_4>=0$$

2. Solve the following LPP by using the dual simplex method

Minimize $Z=10X_1+6X_2+2X_3$

STC

$$-X_1+X_2+X_3>=1$$
$$3X_1+5X_2-X_3>=2$$
$$X_1, X_2, X_3>=0$$

3. Using the dual simplex method solve the following LPP:

Minimize $Z=3X_1+2X_2+X_3+4X_4$

STC

$$2X_1+4X_2+5X_3+X_4>=10$$
$$3X_1-X_2+5X_3-2X_4>=2$$
$$5X_1+2X_2+X_3+6X_4>=15$$
$$X_1, X_2, X_3, X_4>=0$$

4. Use duality in obtaining an optimum solution to the following LPP:

Maximum $Z=3X_1+2X_2$

STC

$X_1+X_2 >=1$

$X_1+X_2 <=7$

$X_1+2X_2 <=10$

$X_2 <=3$

$X_1, X_2, >=0$

5. Write the dual of the following LPP:

Minimize $Z=X_1+X_2+X_3$

STC

$X_1+X_2+X_3 =5$

$X_1+X_2 <=3$

$2X_1-X_3 >=4$

$X_1, X_2, >=0$ and X_3 is unrestricted.

6. Using the dual of the following LPP:

Minimize $Z=3X_1+5X_2+6X_3$

STC

$X_1+4X_2+6X_3 <=5$

$2X_1+3X_2+5X_3 >=4$

$3X_1+X_2+7X_3 =3$

$X_1, X_2, >=0$ and X_3 is unrestricted

7. Construct the dual of the problem

Maximum $Z=4X_1+5X_2+12X_3$

STC

$2X_1+X_2+X_3 <=4$

$3X_1-2X_2+X_3 =3$

$X_1, X_2, X_3 >=0$

8. Using duality, find the optimal solution to the problem.

Maximum $Z=4X_1+2X_2$

STC

$X_1-2X_2>=2$

$X_1+2X_2=8$

$X_1-X_2<=10$

$X_1>=0$, X_2 is unrestricted

9. Write down the dual of the following LPP

Minimize $Z=3X_1-2X_2+4X_3$

STC

$2X_1+3X_2-X_3<=8$

$6X_1+7X_2+4X_3>=-10$

$3X_1+2X_2+X_3=7$

$X_1, X_2>=0$, X_3 is a unrestricted variable

10. Solve the following LPP using the dual read-off technique:

Minimize $Z=10X_1+6X_2$

STC

$X_1+X_2>=10$

$2X_1-X_2<=-3$

$X_1+2X_2>=15$

$4X_1+3X_2>=25$

$X_1, X_2, >=0$

11. Give the dual of the following LPP

Maximum $Z=5X_1+6X_2$

STC

$X_1+2X_2<=5$

$-X_1+5X_2>=3$

$4X_1+7X_2<=8$

$X_1, X_2, >=0$

12. Solve the following LPP using the dual simplex method:

Minimize $Z = 2X_1+2X_2+4X_3$

STC

$2X_1+3X_2+5X_3 <= 2$

$3X_1+X_2+7X_3 <= 5$

$X_1-4X_2-6X_3 <= -3$

$X_1, X_2, X_3 >= 0$

13. Solve by dual simplex

Minimize $Z=10X_1+6X_2+2X_3$

STC

$-X_1+X_2+X_3 >= 1$

$3X_1+X_2-X_3 >= 2$

$X_1, X_2, X_3 >= 0$

14. Write the dual of the following LPP:

Minimize $Z=2X_1+3X_2+4X_3$

STC

$2X_1+3X_2+5X_3 >= 2$

$3X_1+X_2+7X_3 = 3$

$X_1+4X_2+6X_3 <= 5$

$X_1, X_2 >= 0$ and X_3 is unrestricted.

15. Solve the following using dual simplex method.

Minimize $Z=X_1+2X_2+3X_3$

STC

$2X_1-X_2+X_3 >= 4$

$X_1+X_2+2X_3 <= 8$

$X_2-X_3 >= 2$

$X_1, X_2, X_3 >= 0$

16. Write the dual of the following LPP. Find the values of $X_1, X_2,$ and X_3 by solving the dual problem formed.

Maximum $Z= -40X_1+30X_2+60X_3$

STC

$X_1-3X_2-4X_3>= -20$

$-2X_1+X_2+3X_3<=10$

$X_{1,}X_3>=0$ and X_2 is a unrestricted variable.

17. Solve the following LPP as dual simplex method

Minimize $Z=20X0 + 16Y$

STC

$X+Y >=12$

$2X+Y>=17$

$2X>=5$

$Y>=6$

$X,Y>=0$

18. Write the dual for the primal given below:

Maximum $Z=2X_2+5X_3+X_1$

STC

$X_1+2X_3 >=4$

$3X_1+3X_2+18X_3<= 18$

$2X_1-2X_2+6X_3= 8$

$X_{1,}X_2>=0$, X_3 is unrestricted

19. Solve by dual simplex method

Minimize $Z= 6P_1+7P_2+3P_3+5P_4$

STC

$5P_1+6P_2-3P_3+4P_4 >=12$

$P_2-5P_3-6P_4 >= 10$

$2P_1+5P_2+X_3+P_4 >= 8$

$P_{1,}P_{2,}P_{3,}P_4 >=0$

20. Obtain the dual of the following LPP

Maximum $Z=3X_1+X_2+X_3-X_4$

STC

$X_1+5X_2+3X_3+4X_4 <=5$

$X_1+X_2 = -15$

$X_3-X_4 <= -5$

$X_1, X_2, X_3, X_4 >=0$

21. Construct the dual to the primal problem

Minimize $Z=X_1+X_2$

STC

$X_1+X_2 >=15$

$X_1-X_2 <=3$

$2X_1+5X_2 <=20$

$-X_1+ 3X_2 <=10$

$X_1, X_2, >=0$

Then solve the dual problem and read the solutions to the primal.

22. Write the dual of the following LPP, find the values of $X_1, X_2,$ and X_3 by solving the dual problem formed.

Maximum $Z=40X_1+30X_2+60X_3$

STC

$X_1-3X_2-4X_3 >= -20$

$-2X_1+X_2+3X_3 <=10$

$X_1, X_3 >=0$, X_2 is a unrestricted variable

23. Write the dual of the following LPP

Minimize $Z = 2X_1+3X_2+4X_3$

STC

$2X_1+3X_2+5X_3 >=4$

$3X_1+X_2+7X_3 = 6$

$X_1+4X_2+4X_3 <= 12$

$X_1, X_2 >=0$, X_3 is unrestricted

24. Solve the following LPP by dual simplex method:

Minimize $= X_1+2X_2+3X_3$

STC

$$2X_1-X_2+X_3 >= 4$$
$$X_1 + X_2 +3X_3 <= 8$$
$$X_2-X_3 >= 2$$
$$X_1, X_2, X_3 >=0$$

25. State the dual of the following LPP and find the solution of the given LPP by solving its dual:

Minimize $= 2X_1+9X_2+X_3$

STC

$$X_1+4X_2+2X_3 >= 5$$
$$3X_1 + X_2 +2X_3 >= 4$$
$$X_1, X_2, X_3 >=0$$

26. Write down the dual of the following problem

Maximum $Z=2X_1+3X_2$

STC

$$5X_1+2X_2 <=40$$
$$6X_1+12X_2 <=80$$

X_1, X_2 are unrestricted in sign.

27. Solve the following LPP using the result of its dual problem

Minimize $Z=24X_1+30X_2$

STC

$$2X_1+3X_2 >=1$$
$$4X_1+9X_2 >=15$$
$$6X_1+4X_2 <=20$$
$$2X_2 <=3$$
$$X_1, X_2, >=0$$

28. Use dual simplex to solve the following

Minimize $Z=3X_1+30X_2$

STC

$X_1+X_2 >=1$

$2X_1+3X_2>=2$

$X_1, X_2, >=0$

29. Write the dual of the following LPP:

Maximum $Z=15X_1+20X_2$

STC

$X_1+X_3 >= 10$

$3X_1+2X_2>=150$

$X_1 - 3X_2 <= 25$

$-2X_1 + 5X_2 = 65$

$X_{1,} X_2 >=0$

30. Construct the dual to the primal problem.

Maximum $Z = 3X_1+5X_2$

STC

$2X_1+6X_2 <=50$

$3X_1+2X_2<=35$

$5X_1-3X_2 <=10$

$X_2<=20$

$X_1, X_2, >=0$

Then solve the dual problem and read the solution to the primal.

31. Use duality theory and solve the following LPP:

Minimize $Z = 10x_1 + 6x_2 + 2x_3$

s.t., $-x_1 + x_2 + x^3 > 1$

$3x_1 + x_2 - x_3 > 2$

$X_i > 0$

32. Write the dual of the following LPP

Minimum $3x_1 + 5x_2 + 6x_3$

Subject to:

$$X_1 + 4x_2 + 6x_3 < 5$$
$$2x_1 + 3x_2 + 5x_3 > 4$$
$$3x_1 + x_2 + 7x_3 = 3$$
$$x_1\ x_2 > 0 \text{ ; and } x_3 \text{ is unrestricted.}$$

33. Illustrate the following problem with a graph and explain the special feature.

Maximum $Z = 2x_1 + x_2$

Subject to

$$X_1 - x_2 < 10$$
$$2x_2 < 40$$
$$x_1, x_2 > 0$$

34. Show that both the primal and dual programs have the same optimal value for Z and that the solution of each is embedded in the final simplex table of the other for the following LPP.

Minimize $Z = 10w_1 + 6w_2 + 8w_3$

STC

$$w_1 + w_2 + 2w_3 > 2$$
$$5w_1 + 3w_2 + 2w_3 > 1$$
$$w_1, w_2, w_3 > 0$$

35. Write the dual of the following LPP

Maximum $Z = x_1 - x_2 + 3x_3$

Subject to

$$x_1 + x_2 + x_3 < 10$$
$$2x_1 - x_3 < 2$$
$$2x_1 - 2x_2 + 3x_3 < 6$$
$$X_1, x_2, x_3 > 0$$

Solve the dual LPP be simplex method.

36. Write the dual of the following LPP:

Maximum $Z = 3x_1 + 5x_2 - x_3$

s.t. $x_1 + 2x_2 + x_3 < 10$

$3x_1 + 5x_2 - x_3 > -18$

$X_1 > 0$

X_2 is unrestricted

37. Use duality to solve the following LPP:

Minimize $Z = 3x_1 + 5x_2$

s.t. $x_1 + 3x_2 > 24$

$x_1 - 2x_2 > 6$

$4x_1 + 3x_2 > 42$

$X_i > 0$ for all i

38. Write the dual of

Maximum $Z = 3x_1 + 4x_2$

Subject to

$3x_1 + 2x_2 < 14$

$4x_1 + 12x_2 < 21$

$X_1, x_2 > 0$

39. Give the dual of the following LPP and hence solve it.

$X_1 <= 4$

$X_1 <= 6$

$X_1 + X_2 <= 5$

$-X_2 <= -1$

$X_1, X_2 >= 0$

Maximum $Z = 3x_1 - 2x_2$

40. Write down the primal problem to the following dual problem

Maximum $W_1 + W_2 + W_3$

Subject to

$2W_1 + W_2 + 2W_3 <= 2$

$4W_1 + 2W_2 + W_3 <= 2$

$W_1, W_2, W_3 >= 0$

41. Solve the following LPP by using the dual simplex method:

Minimize $Z=10X_1+6\ X_2+2\ X_3$

STC

$-X_1+X_2+X_3>=1$

$3X_1+5X_2-X_3>=2$

$X_1, X_2, X_3>=0$

42. Use duality in obtaining an optimum solution to the following LPP:

Maximum $Z=3X_1+2X_2$

STC

$X_1+X_2\ >=1$

$X_1+X_2\ <=7$

$X_1+2X_2<=10$

$X_2<=3$

$X_1, X_2, >=0$

43. Using the dual of the following LPP:

Minimize $Z=3X_1+5X_2+6X_3$

STC

$X_1+4X_2+6X_3<=5$

$2X_1+3X_2+5X_3>=4$

$3X_1+X_2+7X_3\ =3$

$X_1, X_2, >=0$, X_3 is unrestricted

44. Construct the dual of the problem

Maximum $Z=4X_1+5X_2+12X_3$

STC

$2X_1+X_2+X_3<=4$

$3X_1-2X_2+X_3\ =3$

$X_1, X_2, X_3>=0$

45. Using duality, find the optimal solution to the problem.

Maximum $Z=4X_1+2X_2$

STC

$X_1-2X_2>=2$

$X_1+2X_2=8$

$X_1-X_2<=10$

$X_1>=0$, X_2 is unrestricted

46. Write the dual of the following LPP:

Minimize $Z=X_1+X_2+X_3$

STC

$X_1+X_2+X_3=5$

$X_1+X_2<=3$

$2X_1-X_3>=4$

$X_1, X_2, >=0$, X_3 is unrestricted.

47. Write down the dual of the following LPP

Minimize $Z=3X_1-2X_2+4X_3$

STC

$2X_1+3X_2-X_3<=8$

$6X_1+7X_2+4X_3>=-10$

$3X_1+2X_2+X_3=7$

$X_1, X_2>=0$, X_3 is unrestricted variable.

48. Solve the following LPP using the dual read-off technique:

Minimize $Z=10X_1+6X_2$

STC

$X_1+X_2>=10$

$2X_1-X_2<=-3$

$X_1+2X_2>=15$

$4X_1+3X_2>=25$

$X_1, X_2, >=0$

49. Give the dual of the following LPP

Maximum $Z=5X_1+6X_2$

STC

$$X_1+2X_2 <=5$$
$$-X_1+5X_2 >= 3$$
$$4X_1+7X_2 <=8$$
$$X_1, X_2, >=0$$

50. Solve the following LPP using the dual simplex method:

Minimize $Z = 2X_1+2 X_2+4X_3$

STC

$$2X_1+3X_2+5X_3 <=2$$
$$3X_1+X_2+7X_3 <= 5$$
$$X_1-4X_2-6X_3 <= -3$$
$$X_1, X_2, X_3 >=0$$

51. Solve by dual simplex

Minimize $Z=10X_1+6X_2+2X_3$

STC

$$-X_1+X_2+X_3 >=1$$
$$3X_1+X_2-X_3 >= 2$$
$$X_1, X_2, X_3 >=0$$

52. Write the dual of the following LPP:

Minimize $Z=2X_1+3X_2+4X_3$

STC

$$2X_1+3X_2+5X_3 >=2$$
$$3X_1+X_2+7X_3 = 3$$
$$X_1+4X_2+6X_3 <= 5$$
$$X_1, X_2 >=0,\ X_3 \text{ is unrestricted.}$$

53. Solve the following using dual simplex method.

Minimize $Z=X_1+2X_2+3X_3$

STC

$2X_1-X_2+X_3>=4$

$X_1+X_2+2X_3<=8$

$X_2-X_3>=2$

$X_1, X_2, X_3>=0$

54. Write the dual of the following LPP. Find the values of $X_1, X_2,$ and X_3 by solving the dual problem formed.

Maximum $Z=-40X_1+30X_2+60X_3$

STC

$X_1-3X_2-4X_3>=-20$

$-2X_1+X_2+3X_3<=10$

$X_1, X_3>=0$ and X_2 is unrestricted variable.

55. Solve the following LPP as dual simplex method

Minimize $Z=20X0+16Y$

STC

$X+Y>=12$

$2X+Y>=17$

$2X>=5$

$Y>=6$

$X,Y>=0$

56. Write the dual for the primal given below:

Maximum $Z=2X_2+5X_3+X_1$

STC

$X_1+2X_3>=4$

$3X_1+3X_2+18X_3<=18$

$2X_1-2X_2+6X_3=8$

$X_1, X_2>=0$, X_3 is unrestricted

57. Obtain the dual of the following LPP

Maximum $Z=3X_1+X_2+X_3-X_4$

STC

$X_1+5X_2+3X_3+4X_4 <=5$

$X_1+X_2 => -15$

$X_3-X_4 <= -5$

$X_1, X_2, X_3, X_4 >=0$

58. Construct the dual to the primal problem

Minimize $Z=X_1+X_2$

STC

$X_1+X_2 >=15$

$X_1-X_2 <=3$

$2X_1+5X_2 <=20$

$-X_1+3X_2 <=10$

$X_1, X_2, >=0$

Then solve the dual problem and read the solutions to the primal.

59. Write the dual of the following LPP. Find the values of X_1, X_2, and X_3 by solving the dual problem formed.

Maximum $Z=40X_1+30X_2+60X_3$

STC

$X_1-3X_2-4X_3 >= -20$

$-2X_1+X_2+3X_3 <=10$

$X_1, X_3 >=0$, X_2 is a unrestricted variable.

60. Write the dual of the following LPP

Minimize $Z = 2X_1+3X_2+4X_3$

STC

$2X_1+3X_2+5X_3 >=4$

$3X_1+X_2+7X_3 = 6$

$X_1+4X_2+4X_3 <= 12$

$X_1, X_2 >=0$, X_3 is unrestricted

61. State the dual of the following LPP and find the solution of the given LPP by solving its dual:

Minimize = $2X_1+9X_2+X_3$

STC

$$X_1+4X_2+2X_3 >= 5$$
$$3X_1+X_2+2X_3 >= 4$$
$$X_1, X_2, X_3 >= 0$$

62. Write down the dual of the following problem

Maximum $Z=2X_1+3X_2$

STC

$$5X_1+2X_2 <= 40$$
$$6X_1+12X_2 <= 80$$

X_1 and X_2 are unrestricted in sign

63. Write the dual of the following LPP

Maximum $Z=15X_1+20X_2$

STC

$$X_1+X_3 >= 10$$
$$3X_1+2X_2 >= 150$$
$$X_1 - 3X_2 <= 25$$
$$-2X_1+5X_2 => 65$$
$$X_1, X_2 >= 0$$

5

Transportation Problems

INTRODUCTION

The transportation model is a special case of linear programming that deals with shipping a commodity from sources to destinations (factories to warehouses). The objective of transportation model is to determine the shipping schedule that minimises the total shipping cost while satisfying supply and demand limitations.

The model assumes that the shipping cost is proportional to the number of units shipped on a given route. The transportation can be extended to the areas of operation, inventory control and employment scheduling and personnel assignment.

The transportation model can be solved as a regular linear programming; its special structure allows the development of a simplex based computational algorithm that makes use of the primal-dual relationships to simplify the computations. The transportation problems actually are special cases of the minimum cost flow problem and can be used for network representation of the transportation. The transportation problem involves 'm' sources each of which are available a_i (i-1, 2, ...m) units of a homogeneous product and 'n' destinations each of which requires b_j, (j = 1, 2, ... n) units of this product. The numbers 'a' and 'b', are positive integers. The cost of C_i of transporting one unit of product from the ith source to the jth destination is given for each i and j. The objective is to develop an integral transportation schedule that meets all demands from current inventory at a minimum total shipping cost; it is assumed that total supply and total demand are equal.

$$\sum_{i=1}^{n} a_i = \sum_{i=1}^{n} a_i$$

The transportation algorithm is the simplex method specialized to the format and it involves:

- Finding an initial basic feasible solution.
- Testing the solution for optimality.
- Improving the solution when it is not optimal.

The goal is to allocate the supply available for each origin so as to optimize a criterion while satisfying the demand at each destination. The usual objective function is to minimise the total transportation cost or total weighted distance or to maximize the total profit contribution from the allocation.

Applications

- To minimize the sum of shortage and shipping costs.
- To minimize purchase and shipping cost.
- To minimize the daily cost of processing checks.
- To maximize the revenue.

Transportation Problems

1. The figures in the body of table below are proportional to the cost of transportation of the tonne of food grain from the part given by row heading to the destination given by column heading. Find the optimum distribution schedule to minimize the transportation cost.

Ports	Delhi	Hyderabad	Mysore	Nagpur	Stock in (1000 tonnes)
Bombay	9	5	8	5	225
Calcutta	9	10	13	7	75
Madras	14	5	3	7	100
Requirement in 1000 tonnes	125	80	95	100	

2. A company has factories A, B and C which supply warehouses at D, E, F and G. Monthly factory capacities are 250, 300 and 400 units respectively for regular production. If overtime production is utilized, factories A and B can produce 50 and 75 additional units respectively at overtime incremental costs of Rs. 4 and Rs. 5 respectively. The current warehouse requirements are 200, 225, 275 and 300 units respectively. Transportations cost of these units (in Rs.) from factories to warehouses are as follows.

		To			
		D	E	F	G
From	A	11	13	17	14
	B	16	18	14	10
	C	21	24	13	10

Determine the optimum distribution for this company to minimize cost. (Use VAM to find initial basic feasible solution and MODI method for optimality test.)

3. Freshwater is supplied through three reservoirs with daily supply capacities of 15, 20 and 25 million liters of freshwater respectively. On each day supply must be provided to four cities A, B, C and D whose demands are 8, 10, 12 and 15 million liters is given below:

		Cities			
		A	**B**	**C**	**D**
	1	2	3	4	5
Reservoirs	2	3	2	5	2
	3	4	1	5	2

Use the transportation algorithm to determine the cheapest pumping schedule, if excess water can be disposed of at no cost.

4. A scientist lives in town B and has to be in town A next Sunday. On each of the days Thursday, Friday and Saturday he can give one talk in any of the towns A, B, C expect that he cannot talk in town B on Friday. (He can give more than one talk in the same town. These talks must be on different days.) The fee offered to him for one talk is Rs.120 in A, Rs. 160 in B and Rs. 190 in C plus expense for an overnight stay in a town where he gave his talk. Where should he spend the last three days and nights of the week so as to maximize his income from talks less the cost of travel between towns? Travel costs are given in the table below.

		To		
		A	**B**	**C**
	A	—	50	20
From	B	50	—	70
	C	20	70	—

5. Solve the following transportation problem. The demand at destination 1 must be shipped only from Source 4.

	D_1	D_2	D_3	Availability
S_1	5	1	0	20
S_2	3	2	4	10
S_3	7	5	2	15
S_4	9	6	0	15
Requirement	5	10	15	

The entries in the table give the cost of transportation of one unit from source S_1 to destination D_j.

6. A company with fractions A, B, C and D supply warehouses E, F, G and H. The monthly capacities of factories are 80, 100, 120 and 190 for A, B, C and D respectively. The monthly requirements are 110, 90, 150 and 130 for E, F, G and H respectively. The unit transportation costs are given in the table below. The profit per unit excluding transportation cost are Rs. 70, Rs. 50, Rs. 60 and Rs. 90 at factory A, B, C and D respectively. Find the maximum profit production distribution schedule.

Warehouse/ Factory	E	F	G	H
A	15	20	25	30
B	10	40	30	35
C	20	15	40	30
D	30	25	20	30

7. A readymade shop wishes to purchase the dresses from different manufacturers. Determine, how should the order be placed for dresses, so as to maximize the profit. Given the following data.

Types of dress/ Manuf.	A	B	C	D	E	Total quantity available
W	22	28	34	18	12	300
X	24	26	36	14	8	250
Y	20	28	38	16	9	150
Z	26	22	32	20	14	200
Quantity required	150	100	75	250	200	

8. A firm produces a component and distributers them to 5 wholesalers at a fixed price of Rs. 10/unit. Sales forecast indicate that monthly demand will be 3000, 3000, 1000, 5000 and 4000 units at wholesale dealers a, b, c, d and e respectively. The monthly production capacities are 5,000, 1,000 and 10,000 at plants A, B and C respectively. The production costs per unit are Rs. 2, Re. 1 and Rs. 3 at plants A, B and C respectively. The unit transportation cost in rupees between the plants and wholesalers are given in the following table:

	Wholesalers				
Plants	**a**	**b**	**c**	**d**	**e**
A	0.5	0.5	1.0	1.5	1.5
B	1.0	0.5	1.0	1.0	1.5
C	1.0	1.0	0.5	1.5	1.0

Determine the transportation schedule between plants and wholesalers in order to maximize the total profit per month. Use VAM to obtain the initial basic feasible solution.

9. A plant has four main work centers at which end items are reassembled. Each centre uses a common part this is stored in three different locations. The table summarizes the distances (in meters) between each bin and each work centre, the number of parts available in each bin and the number required at each work centre.

	Work centre				
Bins	**1**	**2**	**3**	**4**	**Parts available**
1	25	40	75	20	2000
2	50	40	65	25	1500
3	25	50	70	40	1500
Parts required	800	1200	1500	1000	

Further exactly 500 parts must be delivered to work centre 3 to bin 2 and at least 400 parts from bin 1 to work centre 4. If the objective is to minimize the weighted measure of volume of parts multiplied by the distance in meters, then, formulate the problem as a transportation model with all the constraints and find the optimal solution after obtaining initial solution by VAM.

10. A company has factories A, B and C which supply warehouses at D, E, F and G. Monthly factory capacities are 150, 200 and 250 units respectively for regular production. If overtime production is utilized, factories A and B can produce 50 and 100 additional units respectively. The current requirements of warehouses are 300, 200 and 200 units respectively. The expected profit/unit for different combinations of factories to the warehouses are given below. If overtime is utilized, the expected profit/unit is decreased by Rs. 4 and Rs. 5 for A and B respectively. Determine the optimum and the maximum profit.

	D	E	F
A	11	13	17
B	16	18	14
C	21	20	23

Ans: 12,700

11. Consider the following unbalanced transportation problem.

		To			
		1	2	3	Supply
	1	5	1	7	10
From	2	6	4	6	80
	3	3	2	5	15
	Demand	75	20	50	

Since there is not enough supply, some of the demands at these destinations may not be satisfied. Suppose there are penatly costs for every unsatisfied demand unit which are given by 5 and 3 for destinations 1 and 2 respectively, but the demand at destination 3 must be satisfied. Find the optimal solution starting from the feasible solution obtained by North West corner method. Does the problems have alternate solution? If so, justify.

12. An airfreight company picks up and delivers freight where customers require. Company has two types of aircraft X and Y with equal loading capacities but different operating costs which are as shown below:

Type of aircraft	Cost per km (Rs.)	
	Empty	Loaded
X	1.00	2.00
Y	1.50	3.00

The present four locations of the aircraft which the company is having are as shown below:

J—X   K—Y   L—Y   M—X

Four customers of the company located at A, B, C and D want to transport nearly the same size of load to their final destinations. The final destinations are at a distance of 600, 300, 1000 and 500 km from the loading points A, B, C and D respectively. Distance in kilometers between locations of aircraft and the loading points are as follows:

		Loading Points			
		A	B	C	D
Present location of aircraft	J	300	200	400	100
	K	300	100	300	300
	L	400	100	100	400
	M	200	200	300	200

Determine the optimal allocations.

13. Find the optimal solution for the following transportation problem. Use Vogel's approximate method to find the initial table. Verify for optimality.

		Destination				
		A	B	C	D	Available
Source	I	21	16	25	13	11
	II	17	18	14	23	13
	III	32	10	22	45	19
	Requirement	6	10	12	15	

14. Solve the following transportation problem.

		Destination			
		X	**Y**	**Z**	**Supply**
	A	1	2	6	7
Source	B	0	4	2	12
	C	3	1	5	11
	Demand	10	10	10	

The entry in the box gives the unit cost transportation.

15. Power station P_j, j = 1, 2, 3, 4 run on coal found in coal mines Q_i, i = 1, 2, 3. Quantity of coal produced at Q_i is a_i—maximum possible production of power at P_j is b_j. The cost of unit quantity of coal at Q_i is C_i and its transportation cost to P_j is C_{ij}. A unit quantity of coal produces h_j units of power at P_j. How should coal be distributed so that the total cost of coal at power stations is minimum? How much of power is produced at each station? Solve the problem for the following data.

i	C_{i1}	C_{i2}	C_{i3}	C_{i4}	C_i	a_i
1	4	3	2	1	10	750
2	3	5	6	2	15	350
3	0	4	3	3	20	400
h_j	1/2	1/2	1/3	1/4	—	—
b_j	100	150	300	200	—	—
j	1	2	3	4	—	—

16. Hindustan Construction Company needs respectively 3, 3, 4 and 5 million cubic feet of fill at four earthen dam-sites I, II, III and IV in Punjab. It can transfer the fill from three mounds A, B and C where 2, 6 and 7 million cubic feet of fill is available respectively. Costs of transporting one million cubic feet of fill from mounds to the four sites in lakh are given in the following table.

		To			
		I	**II**	**III**	**IV**
	A	15	10	17	18
From	B	16	13	12	13
	C	12	17	20	11

Determine the optimum transportation plan which minimizes the total transportation cost to the company.

17. A company produces a product in three of its plants. Production costs and raw material costs differ at each plant. The products sale price also differs at different warehouses which are supplied the products by the three plants. The rates of production in plants P_1, P_2 and P_3 are 4, 3 and 7 units per hour respectively.

Plant	Production cost per unit Rs.	Raw material cost/unit Rs.	Capacity hours
P_1	14	12	400
P_2	18	10	400
P_3	13	10	200

Warehouses	Transportation cost/unit (Rs.)			Sales price unit Rs.	Requirement (units)
	P_1	P_2	P_3		
W_1	4	6	5	32	1300
W_2	1	6	4	33	1000
W_3	5	7	3	31	1000
W_4	7	2	9	34	900

- Formulate the transportation matrix with all the constraints.
- Determine optimal shipping pattern using VAM for initial solution.

18. A dealer stocks and sells four types of bicycles which he may procure from different suppliers. His anticipated sales for type A, B C and D for coming season are 410, 680, 318 and 550 numbers. He can obtain from suppliers 1, 2 and 3, 900, 1600 and 560 bicycles respectively. Profit per bicycle in rupees for each supplier and type is as follows:

		Type			
		A	B	C	D
	1	21.5	26	19.5	21
Supplier	2	20.5	24	20	21
	3	18	19.5	19	19.5

Solve the problem for the maximum profit.

19. The following table gives unit cost of transporting a certain material from supply points A, B, C to demand points 1, 2, 3, 4 and supply capacities at A, B, C and demands at 1, 2, 3 and 4.

To/ From	1	2	3	4	Supply capacity
A	5	1	7	10	10
B	6	4	6	5	80
C	3	2	5	8	15
Demand	75	20	50	25	

Due to a previous contractual obligation, a minimum of 5 units of the material must be supplied from A to 4. As there is more demand than supply capacity, demands at some of the demand points cannot be satisfied. There are penalty costs for every unsatisfied demands unit which are given by 5, 3, 2 and 4 for demands points 1, 2, 3 and 4 respectively. Find the optimum schedule of transportation and associated transportation cost. Is the optimum schedule obtained unique one?

20. Solve using VAM

	W_1	W_2	W_3	W_4	Capacity
F_1	21	16	25	13	11
F_2	17	18	14	23	13
F_3	32	27	18	41	19
Requirement	06	10	12	15	43

21. The following table gives the information regarding supply in each warehouse, demand of each market and the unit transportation cost in rupees from each warehouse to each market.

		Market				
		1	2	3	4	Supply
	A	5	2	4	3	22
Warehouse	B	4	8	1	6	15
	C	4	6	7	5	8
	Demand	7	12	17	9	

The shipping clerk has worked out the following schedule: 12 units from A to 2, 1 unit from A to 3, 9 units from A to 4, 15 units from B to 3, 7 units from C to 1 and 1 unit from C to 3.

- Check the solution for optimality.
- Find the optimal solution and cost.
- If the clerk is approached by a carrier of routes A to 1 who offers to reduce his rate in the hope of getting some business, by how much must the rate be reduced before the clerk definitely gives him some business?

22. Solve the following transportation problem and determine the optimal distribution for the company to minimize the shipping cost.

Factories	Warehouses			Available
	W_1	W_2	W_3	
F_1	16	20	12	200
F_2	14	8	18	160
F_3	36	24	16	90
Required	180	120	170	450

23. A firm produces four products A, B, C and D. There are four operators 9 (I, II, III and IV), who are capable of producing any of these products. The processing time varies from operator to operator. The firm records 8 hours of working per day and allows 30 minutes for lunch. The products A, B, C and D gives of Rs. 8, 6, 5 and 4 per product respectively. The processing time for each product is given below find the optimum distribution schedule to maximize profit.

	Products (Processing time in minutes)			
	A	B	C	D
Operators I	15	9	10	6
Operators II	10	6	9	6
Operators III	25	15	15	9
Operators IV	15	9	10	10

24. A company has three plants at locations A, B and C. Which supply to warehouses at D, E, F, G and H. Monthly plant capacities are 800, 500 and 900 units respectively. Monthly warehouses requirements are 400, 400, 500 400 and

800 units respectively. Unit transportation costs in rupees are given below:

		To				
		D	E	F	G	H
	A	5	8	6	6	3
From	B	4	7	7	6	5
	C	8	4	6	6	4

Determine the optimum distribution for the company to minimize the total transportation cost.

25. A electrode manufacturing company has its manufacturing plants located at Thane, Asansol, Gawhati and Faridabad. The market demand necessary is having the warehouses in Calcutta, Bombay, Madras and Delhi. The following table gives the maximum capacities of the respective plants and their requirements of warehouses. The transportation cost per unit is given by.

	C	B	M	D	Capacity
T	3	1	2	2	700
A	1	3	3	3	600
G	2	4	5	3	200
F	3	2	4	1	400
Demand	400	700	300	500	

Ans.: 2,800

26. A chemical corporation has 3 plants A, B and C. Each plant uses a certain chemical that it buys in 100 kg. Requirements for the next three months are plant A 1200 bags, plant B 4800 bags and plant C 3000 bags. Four vendors W, X, Y and Z have agreed to supply these materials. Each has a capacity restriction limiting the total amount he can supply during the next three months. The capacities and selling prices are as follows:

Vendor	Capacity (bags)	Price (Rs./bag)
W	5,000	30/-
X	2,500	25/-
Y	1,200	20/-
Z	1,000	15/-

The cost of shipping from each vendor to each plant are as follows:

Vendor	A	B	C
W	10	5	6
X	4	3	5
Y	1	7	6
Z	4	9	3

Determine the quantities to be purchased from each vendor and where they are to be shipped, so that the plants' overall requirements are met at overall minimum cost.

27. A company has plans to manufacture five products A, B, C, D and E at three plants X, Y, Z. The production capacity the market requirement of production and the production costs are given below:

Plant	Production cost/unit					Production capacity
	A	B	C	D	E	
X	10	15	17	19	16	90
Y	20	12	16	18	20	50
Z	9	14	21	10	18	60
Market requirement	40	50	60	30	70	

Which products should be produced at what levels and at which plant, so as to optimize the total production cost.

28. A company has factories A, B and C which supply warehouses at D, E, F and G. Monthly factory capacities are 160, 150 and 190 units respectively. Monthly warehouse requirements are 80, 90 110 and 160 units respectively. Unit shipping costs (in rupees) are as follows:

		To			
		D	E	F	G
From	A	42	48	38	37
	B	40	49	52	51
	C	39	38	40	43

Determine the optimum distribution for this company to minimize shipping costs.

29. A company wanted to purchase four types of articles (450, 300, 225, 750) and floated the tender. Only three companies responded indicating each can supply only any items required by the company. The company calculated the profit possible by purchasing from each tender as follows:

Tenders	For items			
	A	B	C	D
X	2.5	3.0	4.5	2.25
Y	3.1	3.45	4.3	1.95
Z	2.6	3.85	4.9	2.10

Indicate how order should be placed with tenders to get maximum profit.

30. Explain the terms degeneracy with respect to transportation problem and method of resolving it. Three refineries (A, B, C) having capacity to supply 3, 2, 5 and 4 million litres per day. They are supplying to 3 distribution points where the demands are 2, 4 and 2 million litres per day. The refineries A, B, C are connected by pipe lines (A to B, B to C and C is not linked to A). The cost of transportation of surplus from one to the other are as follows: (cost of per 1000 liters).

Refinery	Distribution point		
	1	2	3
A	240	540	—
B	900	300	240
C	600	750	360

Find the optimal conditions.

31. At beginning of the next week there will be a surplus of 6, 9, 7 and 5 trailers in cities A, B, C and D respectively. Cities E, F and G will have a deficit of 11, 7 and 9 trailers respectively. The cost of moving trailers from each surplus city to each deficit city is given (in rupees) in the following matrix.

		Deficit		
		E	F	G
	A	26	32	28
Surplus	B	19	27	16
	C	39	21	32
	D	18	24	23

Find the minimum cost transportation schedule.

32. A departmental store wishes to purchase the following quantities of dresses:

Dress type	A	B	C	D	E
Quantity	150	100	75	250	200

Tenders are submitted by 4 different manufacturers who have undertaken to supply not more than the quantities below (all types combined).

Manufacturer	W	X	Y	Z
Total quantity	300	250	150	200

The store estimates that its profit per dress will vary with the manufacturer as shown in the matrix below. How should orders be placed?

Manufacturer	Dress type				
	A	B	C	D	E
W	2.75	3.50	4.25	2.25	1.50
X	3.00	3.25	4.50	1.75	1.00
Y	2.50	3.50	4.75	2.00	1.25
Z	3.25	2.75	4.00	2.50	1.75

33. A company has 3 factories from which it transports to four warehouses. The unit cost of production at the three factories are Rs. 4, Rs. 3 and Rs. 5 respectively. Given the following information on unit cost of transportation, capacity at three factories and the requirements of the four warehouses, find the optimum allocation.

	Unit cost of production		Transportation cost		Capacity
	Rs/unit	W_1	W_2	W_3	W_4
F_1	4	5	7	3	8	300
F_2	3	4	6	9	5	500
F_3	5	2	6	4	5	200
Requirements, units		200	300	400	100	

Ans.: 7,900

34. Obtain the optimum solution to the following transportation problem given the matrix of unit costs of transportation:

Sources	Destination			
	A	B	C	D
P	12	11	14	9
Q	6	4	4	8
R	8	6	7	3

The availability at sources P, Q and R are 50, 70 and 120 units respectively, whereas the demands at destination A, B, C and D are 50, 80, 100 and 20 respectively.

35. Solve the following transportation problems

	W_1	W_2	W_3	W_4	Capacity
F_1	8	6	5	4	100
F_2	7	3	9	2	150
F_3	6	5	4	3	175
Demand	75	200	25	125	425/425

So parties who supply the following quantity of

Party 1 = 14 tonnes

Party 2 = 12 tonnes

Party 3 = 5 tonnes

There are 3 consumers who require the coal as follows:

Consumer A= 6 tonnes

Consumer B = 10 tonnes

Consumer C = 15 tonnes

The cost matrix in Rs./tonnes is as follows:

	A	B	C
P_1	6	8	4
P_2	3	9	3
P_3	1	2	6

Find the schedule of transportation policy which minimizes the cost. **Ans. 128**

36. A company has 3 plants supplying the same product to 5 distributing centres. Due to pecularties inherent in the set of cost, the manufacturing cost/unit and transporting from place to place is given. There are restrictions on monthly capacities plant. Each distributing centre has specific requirement capacity. Requirement and cost of transportation are given below.

	1	2	3	4	5	Capacity
A	5	3	3	6	4	200
B	4	5	6	3	7	125
C	2	3	5	2	3	175
Requirement	60	80	85	105	70	

The cost of manufacture of products at different plants

	Variable cost/unit	Fixed cost
A	13	700000
B	15	400000
C	14	500000

Determine the quantity to be dispatched form cost. Plant to the different distributing centres satisfying the requirement at min. cost. **Ans.: 6,520**

37. A company distributes coal from mines to consumers at the least transportation cost that will meet delivery promise. Given the following data find the best distribution of coal.

- 3 mines located at West Bengal, Bihar and Orissa produce 60, 35 and 45 tonnes/week respectively.
- 5 consumers A, B, C, D, E, who require 22, 45, 20, 18 and 35 tonnes per week respectively
- The transportation cost per tonne is given below:

	A	B	C	D	E
W.B.	4	1	3	4	4
BIHAR	2	3	2	2	3
ORISSA	3	5	2	4	4

Ans.: 310

38. A company has 4 factories A, B, C, D which supply to warehouses at E, F, G, H, I. Monthly capacities are 200, 225, 175 and 350 units respectively. Monthly warehouses requirements are 130, 110, 140, 260 and 180 units to repectively. The shipping in Rs. is as follows:

	E	F	G	H	I
A	14	19	32	9	21
B	15	10	18	7	11
C	26	12	13	18	16
D	11	22	14	14	18

Ans.: 89,350

Determine the optimum distribution for the given transportation problem to minimize the shipping cost.

39. A company has 4 factories F1, F2, F3, and F4 manufacturers same product. Production and raw materials are different and given below. The transportation cost to sales departments S1, S2, S3 are also given. Determine the minimum total cost and optimal solution.

	F_1	F_2	F_3	F_4	Requirement
S_1	3	9	5	4	180
S_2	1	7	4	5	120
S_3	5	8	3	6	150
Production capacity	10	180	50	100	

Production cost/ unit	15	18	14	13
Raw material cost/ unit	10	9	12	9

Ans.: 10,500

40. Solve the following transportation problem for optimal solutions, cell entries represent the unit cost of shipping.

	Stores						Availability
Warehouses	9	12	9	6	9	10	5
	7	3	7	7	5	5	6
	6	5	9	11	3	11	2
	6	8	11	2	2	10	9
Requirement of warehouses	4	4	6	2	4	2	

Ans.: 112

41. A job shop makes 3 products A, B, and C and demand for these products is 90, 210 and 120 units per week respectively. The products can be manufactured by any one of the 3 methods 1, 2 and 3. The capacity of the method 1, 2 and 3 is 160, 120 and 140 units/week respectively. The profit in Rs/unit associated with each product and each manufacturing method are as follows.

	1	2	3
A	139	140	137
B	209	207	210
C	254	255	255

Ans.: 87,140

42. A company has 3 factories manufacturing the same products at 5 side agencies in different parts of the country. The production cost differs factory to factory and sales price differ from agency to agency the shipping cost per unit is known given the following data determine the production and distribution schedule most profitable to the company.

	A_1	A_2	A_3	A_4	A_5	Capacity
F_1	3	1	5	7	4	150
F_2	8	7	8	3	6	200
F_3	4	5	3	2	7	125
Requirement	80	100	75	45	125	

Ans.: 3,070

Sales Price / unit				
30	32	31	34	29

Production cost / unit individually	
F_1	20
F_2	22
F_3	18

43. A corporation has a manufacturing plants 1, 2 and 3, which produce 4 different products A, B, C and D at different variable costs at each plant means that the profit for each product varies as tabulated. The capacity of each plant and demand of each product are given.

	A	**B**	**C**	**D**	**Capacity**
1	22	26	20	21	450
2	21	24	20	19	300
3	18	20	19	20	150
Deamand	200	300	150	270	

Ans.: 20,150

Determine the amount of product that should be allowed in each so that the profits are maximized.

44. ABC company has 3 factories and 3 customers as follows. The factory capacities are A-75, B-80, C-70. The customers' requirements are X-50, Y-100 and Z-40. The ABC company can make the following profits/unit.

	X	**Y**	**Z**
A	38	14	26
B	34	23	17
C	5	33	21

Ans.: 5,490

45. Find out the maximum profit distribution schedule with a restriction that no shipment can be made from factory B to customer Y.

	P	**Q**	**R**	**Supply**
A	5	1	4	10
B	6	4	2	80
C	3	2	5	15
Demand	75	20	50	

Since there is not enough supply some of the demands at these destinations may not be satisfied. Suppose those penalty cost for every unsatisfied demand unit which are given by 5, 3 and 2 for destination P, Q and R respectively. Find the optimal solution and cost.

Ans.: 515

46. A departmental store wishes to purchase the following quantity of saree:

Type of saree	A	B	C	D	E
Quantity	150	100	75	250	200

Tenders are submitted by 4 different manufacturers to undertake to supply not more than the quantity mentioned below.

Manufacturer	W	X	Y	Z
Quantity	300	250	150	200

The store estimates that its profit/saree will vary with the manufacturer as shown by the following matrix

	A	**B**	**C**	**D**	**E**
W	275	350	425	225	150
X	300	325	450	175	100
Y	250	350	475	200	125
Z	325	350	475	200	125

Place order so as to maximum the profit **Ans.: 2,06,875**

47. Four factories manufacturing the same product supply to 3 sales departments S1, S2, and S3. The various costs and also the sale prices are given below. Determine the most profitable production and distribution schedule and corresponding profit. The surplus production should be taken to yield zero net profit.

	F_1	**F_2**	**F_3**	**F_4**	**Capacity**
F_1	3	9	5	4	80
F_2	1	7	4	5	120
F_3	5	8	3	6	150
Requirement	10	150	50	100	

Sales	Price / unit	
34	32	31

Production cost / unit	Material cost/ unit
15	10
18	9
14	12
13	9

Ans.: 480

48. A canning company operates two canning plants. Three growers are willing to supply fresh fruits in the following quantity.
Grower 1 – 200 quintals at Rs. 100/quintal
Grower 2 – 300 quintals at Rs. 90/quintal
Grower 3 – 400 quintals at Rs. 80/quintal
Shipping cost in Rs./quintal are:

	A	B
G_1	20	25
G_2	10	15
G_3	50	30

The plant capacities and labor costs are plant A capacity 450 quintals. Labor cost in Rs./quintal- 250. Plant B capacity 350 quintals. Labor cost in Rs./quintals -200. The canned fruits are sold at Rs. 500/quintals to the distributor. How should the company plan its 2 plants so as to minimize its profit? **Ans.: 1,31,000**

49. Two localized at Bombay and Calcutta should ship their products to warehouses in Cochin, Hyderabad and Madras. Their plant capacities per month are 350 tonnes at Bombay and 650 tonnes at Calcutta. The requirements per month are 300 tonnes each at Cochin, Hyderabad and Madras. The shipping rates are limited to Bombay to Cochin at Rs. 20/tonne. Calcutta to Madras as Rs. 60/tonne. Calcutta to Hyderabad at Rs. 60/tonne and Cochin to Madras at Rs. 70/tonne. Find the cheapest schedule Bombay to Hyderabad is Rs. 80/tonne Calcutta to Cochin is Rs. 40/tonne. **Ans.: 45,000**

50. A furniture manufacturing company has 3 plants which manufacture 2 principal products, a standard card table and a deluxe card table. Now deluxe card table will be introduced which must be considered in terms of selling prices and cost. The selling prices are standard Rs. 15.25, deluxe – Rs. 19.15 and new deluxe – Rs. 21.95. Sales requirements of 3 models are standard – 450, deluxe – 1050 and new deluxe – 600. Variable cost of the model and plant capacities are given below.

	Standard	Deluxe	New deluxe	Capacity
A	8	8.5	9.25	800
B	7.95	8.6	9.2	600
C	8.1	8.45	9.3	700

Solve this problem by transportation method for greatest contribution. **Ans.: 22,130**

51. Three warehouses supply to five stores. The table below indicates the cost of shipment per unit between the warehouses and stores. Warehouse capacity and requirement of stores. However, a major bridge has been damaged preventing the delivery from warehouse therefore to store 5, with B to store 2 warehouses C to store with their limitations determine the optimal delivery scheme.

	A	B	C	Requirement
S_1	2	4	6	75
S_2	3	8	7	345
S_3	4	3	8	180
S_4	4	6	3	90
S_5	2	6	5	210
Capacity	850	300	450	

Ans.: 3,135

52. A manufacturing company has 3 factories A, B, C which supply products to warehouses. D, E, F, G monthly capacities for factories A, B, C are 250,300 and 400 units for regular production. If overtime is utilized factory A and B can produce 50 and 75 additional units. The unit incremented costs are Rs. 4 and 5 respectively requirement are 200, 225, 275 and 300 units for D, E, F and G respectively. The transportation costs/unit are given in the table below.

From / To	D	E	F	G
A	8	9	10	12
B	6	12	9	8
C	5	14	4	13

Determine the optimal distribution for company to minimize the cost. **Ans.: 12,525**

53. A company has factories at A, B, C which supply products to warehouses at D, E, F and G. The factory capacities are 250, 300 and 200 respectively for regular production. If overtime product is utilized the capacity to be increased to 320, 380 and 200 respectively incremental unit overtime costs are Rs. 6, 5 and 7 per unit respectively. The current warehouses requirements are 180, 190, 220 and 180 respectively. Unit shipping cost in rupees between the factory and warehouses are given below:

	D	E	F	G
A	8	9	10	12
B	6	12	9	8
C	5	14	4	13

Determine the optimal distribution for company to minimize the cost. **Ans.: 5,390**

54. Two companies producing the same product are having the inventories of 11000 and 9000 units. This product is used by two categories of people in 3 cities the estimates of the requirement are shown in the table.

Category / city	1	2	3
Category 1	3250	2600	1950
Category 2	7500	8000	65000

The shipping cost in rupees between the companies and cities are as follows:

Company / city	1	2	3
I	30	30	60
II	10	40	70

Ans.: 4,20,000

Determine a minimum cost shipping schedule.

55. Three refineries with maximum daily capacities of 6, 5, 8 million gallons of gasoline supply to three distribution areas with daily demands of 4, 8, 4 million gallons, through a network of pipelines. The transportation costs per 100 gallons are given below:

	From / To	1	2	3
	1	120	180	—
Refinery	2	300	100	80
	3	200	250	120

Note that refinery 1 is not connected to distribution area 3. Any surplus production at refinery 1 and 2 must be diverted to other areas by trucks, the resulting transportation cost per 100 gallons is Rs. 150 from refinery 1 and Rs. 220 from refinery 2. The refinery 3 can divert its surplus to a chemical process within its own plant at no cost. Formulate the problem as transportation model and find the optimal solution. **Ans.: 2070×10^4**

56. From 3 plants ABC comany supply to three customers C_1 C_2 C_3 the profits expected per unit transported from the three plants to the three customers are given below:

	From/ To	C_1	C_2	C_3
	A	4	1	3
Plants	B	2	3	2
	C	3	5	2

The requirements of the customers are 100, 70 and 120 units respectively and the capacities of the plants A, B and C are 80, 130 and 100 units respectively.

Determine the optimum number of units to be transported from each of the plants to each of the customers. Does this problem have more than one optimum solution? If yes, find all those solutions.

Ans.: 970

57. A production manger has a product, which must be produced to meet a fluctuating demand. He knows the monthly requirements are 900 for the first month, 700 for the second month and 1100 for the third month. This product can be produced either on regular time or on overtime. However, there are two restrictions imposed by technical conditions: regular production cannot exceed 800 items per month and overtime production cannot exceed 500 items. Per month manufacturing cost per item in normal working time varies each month: Rs. 3 in the first month, Rs. 4 in the second month and Rs. 2.50 in the third month. The manufacturing costs for overtime are Rs. 4 in the first month Rs. 5 in the second month and Rs. 3.50 in the third month. Monthly storage cost is Rs. 2 per unit items manufactured but not distributed during the month are kept in stock and distributed next month. There is no initial inventory and no inventory is needed at the end of the 3 months. How should the production manager plan his production? **Ans.: 8,650**

58. A company has three factories A, B and C which supply products to warehouses D, E and F. The expected capacities of these factories are 200, 300 and 400 units per month. If overtime production is utilized, factories A and B can produce additional units of 50 and 60 units respectively. The requirements of the warehouses are 400, 300 and 300 units respectively. The expected profit/unit for different combinations of factories and warehouses are given in the table. The profit/unit decreases by Rs. 2 and Rs. 3 for the factories A and B respectively, when they work overtime.

From/To	D	E	F
A	11	13	17
B	16	18	14
C	21	20	23

Determine the optimum distribution schedule and the corresponding maximum profit. Does this problem have an alternate optimum solution?

59. A car agency has eight outlets in a metropolitan area. They have found from experience that it is best to begin each day with all their cars evenly distributed among the eight outlets, assuming that all 80 cars present suppose that at the end of a particular day the number of cars at the outlets is as follows:

Outlets	A	B	C	D	E	F	G	H
No. of cars	1	11	3	15	20	5	7	18

They wish to transport the cars from the surplus outlets to the deficit outlets to attain an even distribution, the best set of movements is that which has the smallest total distance travelled. The distances in km between the outlets are given below:

	A	B	C	D	E	F	G	H
A	—	13	3	11	12	5	8	7
B		—	11	11	25	16	23	9
C			—	19	11	16	7	15
D				—	31	26	16	3
E					—	4	9	12
F						—	8	9
G							—	14
H								—

Solve this problem by transportation algorithm. **Ans.: 210**

60. Steel is produced and then stored in warehouses in 3 cities:

Warehouse location	Weekly productions (tonnes)
A	150
B	210
C	320

Theses plants supply steel to markets in 4 cities, which have the following demand:

Market location	City1	City2	City3	City4
Weekly demand (tonnes)	130	70	180	240

The following shipping cost per tonne have been estimated.

	From / To	City			
		1	2	3	4
Warehouse	A	140	90	160	180
	B	110	80	70	160
	C	160	120	100	220

Due to truckers strike shipments are presently prohibited from B to city #. Solve the problem using transportation algorithm identify the multiple optimal solutions if any. **Ans.: 82,600**

61. The following table gives the cost of transportation of a certain item from supply points A, B, C, D and E to demand points F, G, H and I.

From / To	F	G	H	I
A	8	10	9	12
B	7	19	3	10
C	4	6	8	7
D	10	3	10	9
E	9	4	6	12

The present transportation schedule is as follows:-

A to F 90 units E to F 10 units

B to G 50 units C to H 40 units

D to I 80 units D to G 20 units

The schedule exhausts the capacities of supply points and fulfills the demand of F, G, H and I.

- is the present schedule optimum? If not, find the optimum solution. **Ans.: 1,770**
- if at least 20 units have to be supplied from B to G determine the optimum solution. **Ans.: 1,730**
- if the cost of transportation from E to G is reduced to Rs. 2/ unit, determine the new optimum solution.

62. Solve the following transportation problem using VAM to find the starting solution. The demand at destination must be shipped from source and unit cost of shipping is shown in the table given below:

From/To		Destination			Capacity
		A	B	C	
	1	5	1	0	20
Source	2	3	2	4	10
	3	7	5	2	15
	4	9	6	0	15
	Demand	5	10	15	

63. A readymade garment shop wishes to purchase the dresses from different manufacturers. Determine, how should the orders be placed for dresses so as to maximize the profit, given the following data:

Manufacturer/ Type of dresses	Profit in Rs. / Dress					Total quantity available
	A	B	C	D	E	
W	22	28	34	18	12	300
X	24	26	36	14	8	250
Y	20	28	38	16	9	150
Z	26	22	32	20	14	200
Total quantity required	150	100	75	250	200	

64. A multi-plant company has three manufacturing plants A, B and C and two markets X and Y. Production costs at A, B and C are Rs. 1500, 1600 and 1700 per piece respectively. Selling price in X and Y are Rs. 4400 and Rs. 4700 respectively. Demands in X and Y are 3500 and 3600 pieces. Production capacities at A, B and C are 2000, 3000 and 4000 pieces respectively. Transportation costs are as shown in the matrix below. Build a mathematical model.

65. Determine the weekly production schedule of a plant for the next 4 weeks so as to minimize the total costs being given that production cost of the item is Rs. 10 for the first 2 weeks and Rs. 15 for the last 2 weeks. The weekly demands are 300, 700, 900 and 800 units of the item which must be satisfied. The plant can produce a maximum of 700 units each week. The company each produces 200 units per week more in 2nd and 3rd week at an extra production cost of Rs. 5 / item. Excess production can be stored at a unit cost of Rs 3/week.

From / To	X	Y
A	1000	1500
B	2000	3000
C	1500	2500

6

Assignment Problems

INTRODUCTION

The best person for the job is a description of the assignment model. The situation can be illustrated by the assignment of workers with varying degrees of skills to jobs. A job that happens to match a worker's skill costs less than that in which the operator is not as skilful. The objective of the model is to determine the least cost (optimum) assignment of workers job.

The assignment model is actually a special type of the transportation model in which the workers represented the sources and its jobs represent the destinations. The supply amount at each destination is equal to one. The cost of transporting worker 'i' to the job 'j' is C_{ij}. The assignment model can be solved directly as a regular transpor-tation model.

The fact that all supply and demand amount equal to one has let to the development of a simple solution algorithm called the Hungarian method. The new method appears totally unrelated to the transportation model. The algorithm is actually rooted in the simplex method just as the transportation model is.

A more efficient way of solving the assignment problem has been developed based on a mathematical property due to the Hungarian method. The basic principle of this method is that the optimal assignment is not affected if a constraint is added or subtracted from any row or column of the standard assignment of cost matrix.

The assignment problem can be solved by the Hungarian Method.

Step 1: The original cost matrix identity each row's minimum and subtract it from all the entries of the row.

Step 2: For the matrix resulting from step 1, identify each column's minimum and subtract it from all the entries of the column.

Step 3: Identify the optimal solution as the feasible assignment associated with the zero elements of the matrix obtained in step 2.

The application of assignment technique is assigning people to tasks, airline departure and arrival of the flights and other areas.

Applications

- To minimize the total time required to compute the jobs.
- To minimize cost assignment of persons to jobs.
- To minimize time for arrival and departure of flights.

Assignment Problems

1. A company has four territories open and four salesmen available for assignment. The factories are not equally rich in their sales potential. It is estimated that a typical salesman operating in each territory would bring in the following annual sales:

Territory	**I**	**II**	**III**	**IV**
Annual sales (Rs.)	**60,000**	**50,000**	**40,000**	**30,000**

The four salesmen are also considered to differ in ability; it is estimated that working under the same conditions, their annual sales will be proportionately as follows:

Salesman	A	B	C	D
Proportion	7	5	5	4

If the criterion is to maximize expected total sales, the intuitive answer is to assign the best salesman to the richest territory, the next best salesman to the second richest and so on. Verify this answer by assignment technique.

2. A batch of four jobs can be assigned to five different machines. The following table gives the setup time for each job on various machines.

		Machines				
		1	**2**	**3**	**4**	**5**
	1	10	11	4	2	8
Job	2	7	11	10	14	12
	3	5	6	9	12	14
	4	13	15	11	10	7

Find the optimal assignment of jobs to machines, which will minimize the total setup time.

3. Solve the following assignment problem (minimization problem).

	a	b	c	d	e
A	160	130	175	190	200
B	135	120	130	160	175
C	140	110	155	170	185
D	50	50	80	80	110
E	55	35	70	80	105

4. The owner of a machine shop has four machinists available to assign to jobs for that day. Five jobs are offered with expected profit for each machinist on each job as follows:

	A	B	C	D	E
1	60	76	48	99	80
2	69	82	59	71	57
3	85	90	109	69	79
4	46	62	85	75	78

Determine the optimum assignment schedule. Which job should be declined?

5. The owner of a small machine shop has four machinists available to assign jobs for the day. Five jobs are offered with the expected time of completion of each job by each machinists as given in the following table. Determine the optimum assignment schedule.

Time in minutes

Jobs/ Operators	**A**	**B**	**C**	**D**	**E**
1	62	78	50	1201	82
2	71	84	61	73	59
3	87	92	100	71	81
4	48	64	87	77	80

Which job is not assigned?

6. Four workers are available to work on four machines and the respective costs associated with each machine worker assignment is given below:

	Machine			
	M_1	M_2	M_3	M_4
W_1	12	3	6	—
W_2	4	10	—	5
W_3	7	2	8	9
W_4	—	7	8	6

The sign (–) indicates that the particular worker machine assignment is not permitted.

(i) Determine the optimum assignment.

(ii) A fifth machine is available to replace one of the existing machines and the associated costs are:

$$w_1 = 4 \text{ Rs.}, w_2 = 3 \text{ Rs.}, w_3 = 3 \text{ Rs. and } w_4 = 2 \text{ Rs.}$$

Determine whether the new machine can be accepted and if so, which machine does it replace?

7. An airline operating seven days a week has a time table as given below. Crew must have a minimum layover time of 5 hrs between flights. Crew can be based either in City A or City B but they must return to their base on a latter flight after they take a flight from their base.

Flight no.	A City	B City
1	6 a.m.	7 a.m.
2	7 a.m.	8 a.m.
3	1.30 p.m.	2.30 p.m.
4	5.30 p.m.	6.30 p.m.

Flight no.	B City	A City
101	7 a.m.	8.15 a.m.
102	7.30 a.m.	8.45 a.m.
103	11.00 a.m.	12.15 p.m.
104	4.30 p.m.	5.45 p.m.

Obtain the pairing of flight that minimizes the layover time away from the base for the crew and also state for each pair where the crew is to be based.

8. A salesman wants to visit cities A, B C, D and E. He does not want to visit any city twice before completing his tour of all the cities and wishes to return to the point of starting journey. Cost of going from one city to another is roughly proportional to the square of distance travelled. Given the following distance matrix find the least cost route for the salesman.

	A	**B**	**C**	**D**	**E**
A	0	2	5	4	1
B	6	0	3	7	3
C	8	6	0	5	2
D	10	4	7	0	6
E	2	1	6	8	0

9. A small airline operating seven days a week serves two cities A and B according to schedule shown in the table below. The minimum layover time between the two flights is 5 hrs. Obtain the best pairing of flights in such a way that the total layover time should be minimum.

Flight no.	**From**	**Departure**	**To**	**Arrival**
1	A	9 a.m.	B	Noon
2	A	10 a.m.	B	1 p.m.
3	A	3 p.m.	B	6 p.m.
4	B	4 a.m.	A	7 a.m.
5	B	11 a.m.	A	2 p.m.
6	B	3 p.m.	A	6 p.m.

10. A firm plans to being production of four new products on its four plants. The unit cost of producing I at plant j is given below. Find the assignment that minimizes the total cost of production per unit.

		Plants			
		1	**2**	**3**	**4**
	A	15	11	13	15
Products	B	17	12	12	13
	C	14	15	10	14
	D	16	13	11	17

11. There are five jobs to be assigned to five operators, the cost table of which is given below:

		Operator				
		1	**2**	**3**	**4**	**5**
Job	1	3	8	2	10	3
	2	8	7	2	9	7
	3	6	4	2	7	5
	4	8	4	2	3	5
	5	9	10	6	9	10

Solve for minimizing the cost.

12. There are four machines and four operators. The assignment costs are given below. The operator I cannot be assigned to machine four. Find the optimal assignment and the corresponding cost.

Machine/ Operator	**1**	**2**	**3**	**4**
I	5	5	—	2
II	7	4	2	3
III	9	3	5	—
IV	7	2	6	7

13. Solve the following travelling salesman problem so as to minimize the cost/cycle.

	C	**D**	**E**	**F**	**G**
C	—	11	11	13	8
D	11	—	5	8	6
E	7	8	—	4	2
F	11	5	4	—	2
G	9	7	4	3	—

14. Solve the following travelling salesman problem. The figures in the matrix indicate time taken in hours to travel between cities:

To/ From	**1**	**2**	**3**	**4**	**5**	**6**
1	—	20	23	27	29	34
2	21	—	19	26	31	24
3	26	28	—	15	36	26
4	25	16	25	—	23	18
5	23	40	13	31	—	10
6	27	18	12	35	16	—

15. A salesman wants to visit cities A, B, C, D and E. He does not want to visit any city twice before completing his tour of all the cities and wishes to return to the point of starting journey. Cost of going from one city to another (in Rs.) is shown in the table below. Find the least cost route.

	A	B	C	D	E
A	0	2	5	7	1
B	6	0	3	8	2
C	8	7	0	4	7
D	12	4	6	0	5
E	1	3	2	2	0

16. A trip from Madras to Bangalore taken six hours by bus. A typical time table of the bus service in both directions is given below:

Madras dept.	Route no.	Bangalore arr.	Madras arr.	Route no.	Bangalore dept.
06.00	a	12.00	11.30	1	05.30
07.30	b	13.30	15.00	2	09.00
11.30	c	17.30	21.00	3	15.00
19.00	d	01.00	00.30	4	18.30
00.30	e	06.30	06.00	5	00.00

The cost of providing service, depends upon the time spent by the bus crew away from their places in addition to service time. There is a constraint that every crew should be provided with more than four hours of rest before the return trip again and should not wait for more than 24 hours for the return trip. Find the assignment of routes to the crew so as to minimize waiting time.

17. A computer centre has got four expert programmers. The centre needs four application programmes to be developed. It was estimated that the computer time in minutes required by each of expert for each of programmes is as follows. Make appropriate assignment to the experts to minimize the total time.

Programmes/ Experts	A	B	C	D
1	120	100	80	90
2	80	90	110	70
3	110	140	120	100
4	90	90	80	90

18. Solve the following travelling salesmen problem.

To/ From	A	B	C	D	E
A	—	40	70	30	40
B	40	—	60	30	40
C	70	60	—	70	50
D	30	30	70	—	70
E	40	40	50	70	—

19. Three jobs A, B, C are to be assigned to 3 machines X, Y, Z. The processing cost per unit for each job-machine combination is shown in matrix. Determine the allocation that minimizes over all processing cost.

	X	Y	Z
A	17	25	31
B	10	15	16
C	12	14	11

Ans. 43

20. A company has 4 machines on which to do three jobs. Each job can be assigned to only one machine. The cost of each job on each machine is given in the table below. What are the jobs assigned that will minimize the costs. What machine should be declined?

	W	X	Y	Z
A	18	24	28	32
B	8	13	17	19
C	10	15	19	22

Ans. 50

21. A gear manufacturing company has received four orders. The company can process these orders in their four departments. The following table gives the profit in rupees, if each order is processed in each department. Due to the constraint in production and delivery schedule the company has to assign one order to one department. To maximize profit out of these orders, which is the best assignment.

	A	B	C	D
1	100	25	160	170
2	125	150	0	80
3	135	105	85	175
4	140	160	180	150

Ans. 635

22. The owner of a machine shop has 4 machines available to the jobs for the day. Five jobs are offered with expected profit in rupees for each machine on each job is follows:

	A	B	C	D	E
1	62	78	50	101	82
2	71	84	61	73	59
3	87	92	111	71	81
4	48	64	87	77	80

Find the assignment of machine to jobs that will result in man profit. What job should be declined. **Ans. 376, A**

23. A group of 5 boys and 4 girls are planning a one-day picnic. The extent of mutual happiness b/w the boys and girls. When they are together is given by following matrix. Data obtained from their previous experiences. The problem is to decide the proper matching b/w the boys and girls during the picnic which will maximize the sum of all the mutual happiness of all couples who will be the spectator.

	G_1	G_2	G_3	G_4
B_1	11	3	5	8
B_2	9	9	8	4
B_3	10	3	5	10
B_4	4	13	12	11
B_5	8	9	10	4

Ans. 44

24. Four machines M_1, M_2, M_3 and M_4 are to be installed on a machine job. There are five vacant places A, B, C, D and E available. Because of limited space, M_2 cannot be placed at C and M_3 cannot be placed at A. The assignment costs of machine to places are given below. Find the optimal assignment schedule.

	A	B	C	D	E
M_1	4	6	10	5	6
M_2	7	4	—	5	4
M_3	—	6	9	6	2
M_4	9	3	7	2	3

Ans. 12

25. A company has five jobs to be done. The following matrix shows the returns in rupees of assigning the jobs to 5 machines to maximize total return.

	A	B	C	D	E
1	5	11	10	12	4
2	2	4	6	3	5
3	3	12	5	14	6
4	6	14	4	11	7
5	7	9	8	12	5

Ans. 50

26. Find the optimal assignment in following matrix.

	1	2	3	4	5
1	11	17	8	16	20
2	9	8	12	6	15
3	13	16	15	12	16
4	21	24	17	28	26
5	14	10	12	11	15

Ans. 60

27. Find the minimum cost for 5*5 assignment problem whose cost co-efficients are given as follows:

	1	**2**	**3**	**4**	**5**
1	– 2	– 4	– 8	– 6	– 1
2	0	– 9	– 5	– 5	– 4
3	– 3	– 8	0	– 2	– 6
4	– 4	– 3	– 1	0	– 3
5	– 9	– 5	– 8	– 9	– 5

Ans. 36

28. An air flight company picks up and delivers flight where customers require, company has two types of aircraft X and Y with equal loading capacity with different operating cost are given below.

Type of aircraft	**Cost/ km in Rs.**	
	Empty	**Loaded**
X	1	2
Y	1.5	3

The present four locations of aircraft are j – x, k – y, l – y, m – x.

Four customers of company at A, B, C and D want to transport the same size of load to their final destination at a distance of 600, 300, 1000 and 500 km respectively. Distance in km between the location of aircraft and loading points are as follows. Determine the location which minimizes the total cost transportation.

	A	**B**	**C**	**D**
J	300	200	400	100
K	300	100	300	300
L	400	100	100	500
M	200	200	400	200

Ans. 6700

29. A company has four plants each of which can manufacture any of the four products. Production costs differ from each other. Sales revenue and cost data are given below. Obtain the data which product each plant should produce to maximize the profit.

	Sales revenue matrix					Production cost matrix			
	1	2	3	4		1	2	3	4
A	50	68	49	62	A	49	60	45	61
B	60	70	51	74	B	65	65	50	69
C	55	67	53	70	C	52	62	53	68
D	58	65	54	69	D	55	63	48	66

Ans. 22

30. A process can be carried out on any of the 6 machines. The average time taken by any operator on any specific machine is given in table. It is proposed to buy a new machine to replace one by existing one and time for operator to carry out the process, on this machine has been estimated and included in table. Is it advantageous at this stage to use the new machine. If so, which of the original machine should be replaced and how should the operator be assigned.

	1	2	3	4	5	6	New
A	10	12	8	10	5	12	11
B	9	10	8	7	8	9	10
C	8	7	8	8	8	6	8
D	12	13	14	14	15	14	11
E	9	9	9	8	8	10	9
F	7	8	9	9	9	8	8

Ans. 47, 49

31. A bank manager has five tellers (T), whom he assigns to customer services (C), foreign exchange notes (N) and savings account (S). Three tellers are not qualified for foreign exchange and 1 teller can't have the notes. The table below indicates the number of customer server 1 hour by the teller. Assuming that manager wishes to serve as many customers as possible. The extra tellers will be assigned to a data processing work.

	C	F	N	S
T_1	60	—	30	50
T_2	70	60	40	50
T_3	30	—	10	30
T_4	40	—	—	60
T_5	40	70	50	80

Ans. 230

32. Five lectures by experts are to be scheduled so as not to conflict with one another. The lectures are to be delivered in the afternoon on weekdays only otherwise because of other schedules certain students will be forced to drop out these lectures. The following table indicates the number of absentees lecturewise and daywise schedule these lectures in such a way so as to minimize the total number of students forced to remain absent.

	L_1	L_2	L_3	L_4	L_5
Monday	3	2	3	9	10
Tuesday	11	5	9	10	2
Wednesday	1	3	8	2	4
Thursday	8	11	10	5	2
Friday	8	6	5	6	9

Ans. 15

33. A small airline operating seven days a week serves two cities A and B according to schedule shown. The layover cost per stop is roughly proportional to the square of layover time. Obtain the pairing of flights that minimizes the layover cost.

Flight no.	Dept. at A	Arr. at B	Flight no.	Dep. at B	Arr. at A
1	9 a.m	12 noon	101	4 a.m	7 a.m
2	10 a.m	1 p.m	102	11 p.m	2 p.m
3	3 p.m	6 p.m	103	3 p.m	6 p.m
4	6 p.m	9 p.m	104	8 p.m	11 p.m

For each pair also mention the city where the aircraft should be based. **Ans. 28**

34. A small airline operating seven days a week serves cities A and B according to schedules shown in the table. The minimum layover time between the two flights is 5 hours. Obtain the best pairing of flights in such a way that total layover time should be minimum.

Flight no.	From	Departure	To	Arrival
1	A	9 a.m.	B	Noon
2	A	10 a.m.	B	1 p.m.
3	A	3 p.m.	B	6 p.m.
4	B	4 a.m.	A	7 a.m.
5	B	11 a.m.	A	2 p.m.
6	B	3 p.m.	A	6 p.m.

35. A company has 4 machines to do three jobs. Each job can be assigned to only one machine. The cost of each job on each machine is given in the table below. What are the jobs assigned that will minimize the costs. What machine should be declined?

	W	X	Y	Z
A	18	24	28	32
B	8	13	17	19
C	10	15	19	22

Answer: 50, 7

36. A national bus service has a surplus of one bus in each of the cities 1, 2, 3, 4, 5 and 6 and a deficit of one bus in each of cities 7, 8, 9, 10, 11 and 12. The distances in miles between the cities are given below. How should the buses be dispatched to minimize total distance travelled.

	7	8	9	10	11	12
1	30	61	28	41	14	40
2	11	18	38	54	70	39
3	16	28	49	40	21	21
4	34	29	37	41	26	32
5	18	29	20	15	19	22
6	71	29	29	49	40	19

Ans. 119

37. The cost matrix of assigning 4 operators on 4 existing machines is given below.

Note: The operator 1 cannot be assigned to machine 3 and operator 3 cannot be assigned to machine 4. A new machine is available whose respective assignment costs are 2, 1, 2 and 8. Determine whether it is economical to replace an existing machine with new one. If the answer is yes, which machine is to be replaced. What should be the savings?

	1	2	3	4
1	5	5	—	2
2	7	4	2	3
3	9	3	5	—
4	7	2	6	7

Ans. 14; 8

38. A new office building has been constructed to allow centralization of administration. Six regional managers will be moved to central location. Each office has the same room area and furnishing, but exposures and views differ. In order to please as many managers as possible, the managers were asked to rank their preferences for office with six being the most desirable and one the least desirable. The rankings are given in table below. Determine the assignment that will give the overall satisfaction.

4	2	5	1	3	6
1	3	5	2	4	6
3	5	6	2	1	4
2	4	6	1	3	5
5	2	6	4	1	3
1	6	3	5	2	4

Ans. 31

39. In a textile sales emporium, 4 salesmen A, B, C, and D are available to handle 4 counters W, X, Y, Z. Each salesman can man one counter. The service time (in hrs) of each counter when manned by each salesman is given below. How should the salesmen be assigned to counter to minimize total service time? Each salesman should handle only one counter.

	A	B	C	D
W	41	72	39	52
X	22	29	49	65
Y	27	39	60	51
Z	45	50	48	52

Ans. 147

40. A college athletics conference has 6 officials. It must assign to 3 conference games. Two officials must be assigned to each game. The conference office desire to assign the officials such that the total distance travelled, by all the 6 officials is minimized. The distances each official would have to travel to each game are given below.

		Game		
		A	B	C
Officials	1	20	45	10
	2	40	90	70
	3	60	70	30
	4	20	60	40
	5	70	15	50
	6	80	25	35

The conference office has decided not to assign official 4 to game A, because of pervious conflicts with the coaches. Determine the optimal assignment. **Ans. 170**

41. On a given day, district headquarters has the information that one ambulance van is stationed at each of the five locations A, B, C, D and E. A dispatch order is to be issued for the ambulance van to reach 6 locations 1, 2, 3, 4, 5 and 6. The distance in km between the present locations of the ambulance vans and destination are given in the table below. Decide the assignment of vans for minimum total distance and also state which destination should not expect ambulance van to arrive.

	1	2	3	4	5	6
A	18	21	31	17	26	29
B	16	20	18	16	21	31
C	30	25	27	26	18	19
D	25	33	45	16	32	20
E	36	30	18	15	31	30

Ans. 89

42. There are five major projects 1, 2, 3, 4 and 5 being contemplated. There are regions A, B, C, D, E and F insisting on allocation of as many number of projects as possible in their region. The state department has evaluated effectiveness of projects in different regions for (i) employment potential. (ii) resource utilization (iii) economic profit ability. (iv) environmental degradation index as tabulated on a 20 point sales as given below.

1. Employment potential

	1	2	3	4	5
A	16	10	8	12	11
B	18	15	12	10	7
C	12	16	12	5	8
D	14	10	3	6	8
E	15	17	11	18	11
F	12	18	11	15	14

2. Resource utilization

	1	2	3	4	5
A	7	6	4	5	3
B	11	4	3	2	1
C	16	5	4	3	2
D	15	3	2	4	1
E	8	3	4	2	4
F	17	5	2	1	3

3. Economic profitability

	1	2	3	4	5
A	11	13	14	15	10
B	10	15	17	11	16
C	13	14	16	12	11
D	7	10	5	11	8
E	10	12	7	11	16
F	5	10	12	13	12

4. Environmental degradation

	1	2	3	4	5
A	15	14	5	3	2
B	13	14	5	3	2
C	12	11	5	4	2
D	12	11	5	4	2
E	9	6	5	4	3
F	6	3	5	5	2

Only one project is to be assigned to each region for minimum total effectiveness. **Ans. 143**

43. A aeroplane company operating 1 day a week in 2 cities A and B according to schedule shown before the layover cost per stop is roughly proportional to square of layover time. They must have a minimum layover of 2 hrs. If the crew are based at city A, how should the crew be assigned to flights so as to minimize total layover cost.

Flight no.	From	Departure	To	Arrival
1	A	8 a.m	B	11 a.m
2	A	9 a.m	B	12 noon
3	A	2 p.m	B	5 p.m
4	A	4 p.m	B	7 p.m
101	B	6 a.m	A	9 a.m
102	B	10 a.m	A	1 p.m
103	B	1 p.m	A	4 p.m
104	B	3 p.m	A	6 p.m

Ans. 407

44. A term of 5 horses and 6 riders have entered a jumping show content.

	R_1	R_2	R_3	R_4	R_5	R_6
H_1	6	4	5	8	2	3
H_2	3	4	8	7	6	2
H_3	5	2	6	3	4	5
H_4	7	9	2	3	4	6
H_5		3	6	8	2	4

The number of penalty points to be expected when each ride any horse is shown below.

How should horses be allotted to riders so as to minimize expected loss of term? Also state reserved rider. **Ans. 12**

45. The owner of a computer shop has four operators available to assign jobs for the day. Five data entry jobs are offered with the expected profit in rupees for each operator on each job being as follows.

Operator	Jobs				
	A	B	C	D	E
1	6.2	7.8	5.0	10.1	8.2
2	7.1	8.4	6.1	7.3	5.9
3	8.7	9.2	11.0	7.1	8.1
4	4.8	6.4	8.7	7.7	8.0

Find the assignment of operators to jobs that will result in maximum profit. If B cannot be assigned to 2 will the assignment change? Find the new maximum profit in this condition for the above problem.

46. The productivity of operators A, B, C and D on different machines M_1, M_2, M_3, M_4 and M_5 in units per shift is given below. Find the optimal assignment.

		Machines				
		M_1	M_2	M_3	M_4	M_5
	A	9	14	10	7	12
Operators	B	8	11	12	—	13
	C	10	10	8	11	—
	D	12	14	11	10	7

47. A company is producing a single product and is selling it through five agencies situated in different cities. All of a sudden there is a demand for the product in another five cities not having any agency of the company. The company is faced with the problem of deciding on how to assign the existing agencies to dispatch the product to needy cities in such a way that the distance travelled is minimum. The distance between the surplus and deficit cities (in kilometers) is given in the table below. Determine the optimum assignment schedule.

		Deficit cities				
		A	B	C	D	E
	I	160	130	175	190	200
Surplus cities	II	135	120	130	160	175
	III	140	110	125	170	185
	IV	50	50	80	80	100
	V	55	35	80	80	105

48. A marketing manager has four salesmen and five sales districts. Considering the capacities for the salesman and nature of the district, the manager estimates that sales per month (in thousands) for each salesman in each district would be as follows:

		District				
		A	B	C	D	E
	1	62	78	50	101	82
Salesman	2	71	84	61	73	59
	3	87	92	111	71	81
	4	48	64	87	77	80

Find the assignment of salesman to district that will result in a maximum sale.

49. Solve the travelling salesman problems, given the following data.

C_{12} =20, C_{13} = 4, C_{14} = 10, C_{23} =5, C_{34} = 6, C_{25} = 10, C_{35} = 6, C_{45} = 20, where Cij = Cji and there is no route between cities i and j if a value for Cij is not shown above.

50. Given the following matrix of setup costs, show how to sequence production so as to minimize setup cost per cycle.

	To				
	A	B	C	D	E
A	—	2	5	7	1
B	6	—	3	8	2
C	8	7	—	4	7
D	12	4	6	—	5
E	1	3	2	8	—

51. (a) Determine the optimum assignment schedule for the assignment problem with the following cost matrix:

	Machines					
Jobs	1	2	3	4	5	6
A	11	17	8	16	20	15
B	9	7	12	6	15	13
C	13	16	15	12	16	8
D	21	24	17	28	26	15
E	14	10	21	11	15	6

(b) If job C cannot be assigned to machine 6 will the optimum solution changed?

52. Six jobs are to be processed using six jigs which are inerasable subject to varying efficiencies of production. The efficiencies achieved on different jobs with respect to jigs is quantified as an index number. A higher number indicates a high efficiency. Obtain an optimal assignment of jobs to jigs so as to maximize efficiency.

	Jigs					
Jobs	**1**	**2**	**3**	**4**	**5**	**6**
1	6	4	4	8	7	—
2	4	1	6	8	—	2
3	—	6	6	4	—	6
4	4	4	6	4	1	3
5	3	—	6	—	—	3
6	2	4	4	6	—	9

Indicate that the jig is not suitable for the job. **Ans. 50**

53. A company has five jobs to be processed which can be done on any of the 6 machines. The following table gives the returns in rupees for various job-machine combinations. Determine the optimum assignment schedule.

	J_1	J_2	J_3	J_4	J_5
M_1	9	22	58	11	19
M_2	43	78	72	50	63
M_3	41	28	91	37	45
M_4	74	42	27	49	39
M_5	36	11	57	22	25
M_6	13	56	53	31	17

Ans. 306

54. Determine the optimum assignment schedule for the following problem. Cost matrix is given as follows.

If the job C cannot be assigned to machine-6, will optimum solution change?

	M_1	M_2	M_3	M_4	M_5	M_6
A	11	17	8	16	20	15
B	9	7	12	6	15	13
C	13	16	15	12	16	8
D	21	24	17	28	26	15
E	14	10	12	11	15	16

Ans. 52

7

Queuing Systems Problems

INTRODUCTION

Queues are a part of everyday life. We all wait in queues to buy a movie ticket, to make bank deposit, pay for groceries, mail a package, obtain a food in a cafeteria, to have ride in an amusement park and have become adjusted to wait but still get annoyed by unusually long waits.

Queuing theory is the study of waiting in all these various activities. It uses queuing models to represent the various types of queuing system that arise in practice. Formulas for each model indicate how the corresponding queuing system proceed perform, including the average amount of waiting that will occur under a variety of circumstances.

The queuing models are very helpful for determining how to operate a queuing system in the most effective way if too much service capacity to operate the system involves excessive costs. The models enable finding an appropriate balance between the cost of service and the amount of waiting.

The flows of materials through manufacturing operations through a sequence of processing stages represent other forms of queues. In this chapter we learn how to construct and solve equations that describe queuing behaviour for a wide variety of situations. We cannot exhaust even the elementary models, because the number of possible variations is enormous. In the terminology of queuing theory, the first proposal involves changing the parameter values of the models but no structural changes.

The second proposal is for a two-server, single queue system and the third is for a two-server separated queue system.

Applications

- Bank teller
- Bank staffing
- Barber shop
- Tool centre
- Service station

Queuing Systems Problems

1. Arrivals at a telephone booth are considerd to be poisson with an average of 10 minutes between one arrival and next. The length of a phone call is assumed to be distributed exponentially with a mean of 3 minutes.

i) What is the probability that a person arriving at the booth will have to wait?

ii) What is the average length of queue that form from time to time?

iii) The telephone company will install a second booth when convinced that an arrival would expect to wait at least 3 minutes for the phone. By how much must the flow of arrivals be increased in order to justify the second booth.

2. A drive in bank window has mean service time 2 mins, while the customers arrive at a rate of six per hour.

Assuming that customers arrive at poisson distribution and service time following exponential distribution

i) What percentage of time will the teller be idle.

ii) After driving up, how long will it take the average customer to wait in line and be served?

What fraction of customers will have to wait in line?

3. The arrival of customers at a banking counter follows poisson distribution with a mean of 45 per hour.

The service rate of the counter clerk also follows poisson distribution with a mean of 60 per hour.

i) What is the probability of having zero customer in the system (P_0)?

ii) What is the probability of having 5 customers in the system? Probability of having 10 customers in the system?

iii) Determine the steady state performance statistics, namely, L_s, L_q, W_s and W_q.

4. In a barber's shop with a single barber, there are three chairs. Out of these one chair is for haircutting and the other two for waiting inside the shop. If there are more than three customers in the shop at any time then three will occupy the chairs and rests wait outside. The customers come according to poisson distribution with average 2 customers per hour. The service time T (per customer) is exponentially with mean 20 minutes.

i) Find the probability that an arriving customer has to wait outside the shop.

ii) Find the probability that an arriving customer gets a chair to sit.

iii) How long is an arriving customer expected to wait before start of service?

iv) How many chairs should be provided so that arriving customer can wait on the chair at least 25 percent of the time?

5. A duplicating machine maintained for office use is used and operated by the secretaries. Since the work to be copied varies in length and copies required, the service rate is randomly distributed but it does approximate poisson with a mean service rate of 10 jobs per hour. The requirements for use are random over the entire 8 hour workday but arrive at a rate of 5 per hour. It is observed that a waiting line develops occasionally. If the time of a secretary is valued at Rs. 3.50 per hour, make an analysis to determine.

i) Machine utilization.

ii) The present of time that an arrival has to wait.

iii) The average system time.

iv) The average cost due to waiting and operating the machine.

6. A servicing center receives jobs on an average of 8 jobs per hour, in poisson fashion. The service time has an exponential distribution with a mean of 6 mins. Determine:

i) The average elapsed time, from the time the job is received until it is completed.

ii) Average number of jobs in the system.

iii) Probability of more than 5 jobs in the system.

iv) Probability that the waiting time for a job is more than half an hour.

v) The proportion of the time that the service centre is idle.

7. A repair shop attended by a single mechanic has an average of four customers an hour who bring small appliances for repair. The mechanic inspects them for defects and quite often can fix them right away or render a diagnosis. It takes him six minutes on the average. Arrivals are poisson and service time has an exponential distribution. Find:

i) The probability of finding at least one customer in the shop.
ii) The average number of customers in the shop.
iii) The average time spent by a customer in the shop.

8. A bank has two tellers working on savings accounts. It has been found that the service time distribution for both deposits and withdrawals are exponential with mean service time of 3 minutes per customer.

Customers are found to arrive in a poisson fashion, with a mean arrival rate of 30 per hour.

i) What is the average waiting time in the system?
ii) What would be the waiting time in the queue if the service time is increased to 4 minutes.

9. At what rate must the clerk of a supermarket work in order to ensure a probability of 0.9 that the customer will not have to wait longer than 12 minutes in the system? It is assumed that the arrivals follows a poisson distribution at rate of 15 per hour. The length of service by the clerk has an exponential distribution.

i) Also find the average number of customer waiting for service.
ii) The probability of having more than 10 customers in the system.

10. At telephone booth in a postoffice arrivals are considered to be poisson with an average inter arrival time of 12 minutes. The length of the phone call is assumed to be exponentially distributed with an average of four minutes. Calculate the following.

i) What is the probability that a fresh arrival will not have to wait?
ii) What is the average length of the queue.
iii) What is the probability that an arrival will have to wait more than 10 minutes before the phone is free.

11. Jobs arrive at a computer center according to a poisson arrival fashion with a mean of 4.5 per hour.

The average time to service a job is 5 min.

i) What is the chance that a new job is straightaway processed?
ii) For what proportion of the time the computer center is idle?

iii) What is the average number of jobs in the center?
iv) What is the average number of jobs waiting?
v) What is the average waiting lines?

12. A one man florist shop has an arrival pattern of 10 customers/hour on a Sunday morning following poisson distribution. The service is FIFO and since the shop has a good reputation, people are ready to wait. The time to serve a customer is 4 minutes and is exponentially distributed. Find:

i) Probability that there is a queue
ii) Average size of the queue
iii) Expected waiting time in the queue
iv) The probability that a customer spends less than 12 minutes in the shop.

13. A self-service store employs one cashier at its counter. Nine customers arrive, on an average, every 5 minutes, while the cashier can serve 10 customers in 5 minutes. Assuming poisson probability distribution for arrival rate and exponential distribution for service rate, find:

i) Average number of customers in the system
ii) Average number of customers in queue
iii) Average time a customer spends in the system
iv) Average time a customer waits before being served.

14. A hospital clinic has a doctor examining every patient brought in for check-up. The doctor averages 4 minutes on each phase of the check-up although the distribution of time spent on each phase is approximately exponential. If each patient goes through the four phases in the check-up and if the arrivals of the patient to the doctor's clinic are approximately poisson at an average of 3 patients per hour, what is the average time spent in examination? What is the most probable time spent for examination?

15. A T.V. repairman finds that the time spent on his jobs has an exponential distribution with mean 20 minutes. If he repairs sets in the order in which they arrive and if the arrival of sets is approximately poisson with an average rate of 15 per 8 hour day, what is the repairman's expected idle time each day? How many jobs are ahead of the average set just brought in?

16. An airport can accommodate three airplanes in 2 minutes for either takeoff or landing. If this rate is poisson, what is the mean time between arrivals for landing or departure to ensure that the average waiting time is 5 minute or less?

17. The men's department of a large store employs one tailor for customer fittings. The number of customers requiring fittings appears to follow a poisson distribution with mean arrival rate 24 per hour. Customers are fitted on a first-come first-served basis, and they are always willing to wait for the tailor's service, because alterations are free. The time it takes to fit a customer appears to be exponentially distributed, with a mean of 2 mins.

i) What is the average number of customers in the fitting room?

ii) How much time a customer is expected to spend in the fitting room?

iii) What percentage of the time is the tailor idle?

18. Customers arrive at a one window drive in bank according to a poisson distribution with mean 10 per hour. Service time per customer is exponential with mean of 5 mins. The space in front of the window including that for serviced car can accommodate a maximum of 3 cars. Other cars can wait outside the space.

i) What is the probability that an arriving customer can drive directly to the space in front of the window.

ii) What is the probability that an arriving customer will have to wait outside the indicated space?

19. In a hair dressing saloon with one barber, the customer arrival follows poisson distribution at an average rate of one every 45 minutes. The service time is exponentially distributed with a mean of 30 minutes. Find:

i) Average number of customers in the saloon.

ii) Average waiting time of a customer before service.

iii) Average idle time of the barber.

20. Arrival at a telephone booth are considered to be poisson at an average time of 8 mins between one arrival and the next. The length of the phone call is distributed exponentially with a mean of 4 mins. Determine:

[a] Expected fraction of the day that the phone will be in use [0.5 units]

[b] Expected number of units in the queue [0.5 units]

[c] Expected waiting time in the queue [0.066 hr]

[d] Expected number of units in the system [1]

[e] Expected waiting time in the system [0.0133]

[f] Expected number of units in the queue that form from time to time

[g] What is the probability that an arrival waits in queue for service?

[h] What is the probability that exactly zero units in the system? [0.5]

[i] Probability that exactly 3 units in the system [0.0625]

[j] Probability that an arrival will not have to wait for service [0.5]

[k] Probability that 3 or more units in the system [0.125]

[l] Probability that an arrival will have to wait more it 6 mins in queue for service [0.236]

[m] Probability that more than 5 units in the system [0.0156]

[n] Probability that an arrival will directly enter for service [0.5]

[o] Probability that an arrival will have to wait more than 8 mins in the system [0.3678]

[p] The telephone company will install a 2nd booth when convinced that an arrival would expect to have to wait for at least 6 mins in the queue for the phone by how much the flow of arrivals be in order to justify a 2nd booth [d = 9]

21. In a self-service store with one cashier, 8 customers arrive on an average of every 5 mins and the cashier can serve 10 in 5 mins. If both arrival and service times are exponentially distributed, then determine.

[a] Average number of customers waiting in the queue for service [3.2]

[b] Expected waiting time in the queue [0.033]

[c] The probability of having more than 6 customers in the system [0.209]

22. Consider a box office ticket window being manned by a single server. Customers arrive to purchase tickets according to poissons input process with a mean rate of 30 hr. The time required to customer has an E.D.with a mean of 90 sec. Determine:

[a] Mean queue length [2.25]

[b] Mean waiting time in the system [0.1]

[c] The probability of the waiting in the queue more than 10 mins [0.146]

[d] The fraction of the time of the server is busy [0.75]

23. A T.V. repairman repairs the sets in the order in which they arrive and expects that the time required to repair a set has an E.D.

with mean 30 mins. The sets arrive in a poisson fashion at an average rate of 10/8 hrs a day.

[a] What is the expected idle time/day for the repair man? [0.375*8]

[b] How many T.V. sets will be a waiting for the repair?

24. In a bank there is only one window. A solitary employee performs all the services required and the window remains open from 7 am to 1 pm. It has been discovered that an average number of clients is 54 during the day and the average service time is 5 mins/person. Find:

[a] Average number of clients in the system [3]

[b] Average waiting time [0.25]

[c] The probability that a client has to spend more than 10 mins in a system [0.60]

25. A departmental secretary recieves an average of 8 job/ hr many are short jobs, while others are quite long, assume however, that the time to perform a job has an ED with a mean of 6 mins. Determine:

[a] The average elapsed time from the time the secretary recieves a job, until it is completed [0.5]

[b] Average number of jobs in the system [4]

[c] The probability that the time in the system is greater than ½ hr [0.3621]

[d] Probability of more than 5 jobs in the system [0.2628]

26. There is a congestion on the platform of a railway station. The trains arrive at the rate of 30/day. The service time for any train is ED with an average of 36 mins, calculate:

[a] The mean queue size [2.25]

[b] The probability that more than 10 trains are in the system [0.0422]

27. The arrival rate for a waiting line system obey a P.D. with a mean of 0.5 units/hr. It is required that the probability of one or more units in the system does not exceed 0.25. What is the minimum service rate that must be provided if the service duration will be distributed exponentially? [2/hr]

28. In a municipality hospital patients arrival are considered to be poisson with an arrival interval time of 10 mins. The doctors (examination and dispensing) time may be assumed to be ED with an average of 6 mins. Find:

[a] What is the chance that a new patient straightaway sees the doctor? [0.4]

[b] For what proportion of the time the doctor if busy? [0.6]

[c] What is the average number of patients in the system? [1.5]

[d] What is the average waiting time of the system? [0.25]

[e] Suppose the municipality wants to recruit another doctor when an average waiting time of an arrival is 30 mins in the queue. Find out how long will it take to justify a 2nd doctor?[d = 8.33]

29. At a one man barber shop customers arrival according to P.D. with a mean arrival rate is 5/hr. The haircutting time is ED with a hair cut taking 10 mins on an average assuming that the customers are always willing to wait. Find:

[a] Average number of customer in the shop [5]

[b] Average waiting time of a customer [0.833]

[c] The percent of time an arrival can walk right without having to wait [16.66%]

[d] The probability of a customer waiting more than 5 mins [0.766]

30. At a stamp vendor window of a postoffice, 20 customers arrive on an average every 10 mins. The vendor clerk can serve 5 customers in 2 mins. Determine:

[a] Average number of customer in the system [4]

[b] Average waiting time of a customers [0.0266]

[c] Probability of a customer waiting more than 3 mins before being served [0.1785]

[d] Idle time of the vendor clerk in a shift of 8 hrs [1.6]

31. Arrival of machinists at a tool crib are considered to be P.D. at an average rate of 6/hr. The length of time the machinist must remain at the tool crib is ED with an average time being 0.05 hr.

[a] What is the probability that the machinist arriving at the tool crib will have to wait [0.3]

[b] What is the average number of machinist at the tool crib [0.428]

[c] The company will install a 2nd tool crib when convinced that a machinist would expect to spent at least 6 mins waiting and being served at the tool crib. By how much the flow of machinist to the tool crib increase to justify the 2nd tool crib [d=10]

32. Jobs arrive at an inspection station according to poisson process at a mean rate of 2/hr and are inspected one at a time on a FIFO basis. The quality control engineer both inspects and makes minor adjustments. The total service time for the job appears to be ED with a mean of 25 mins. Jobs that arrive but cannot be inspected immediately by the engineer must be stored until the engineer is free to take them. Each job requires LM^2 of floor space. Determine:

[a] The waiting line length [4.16]

[b] The waiting time [2.08]

[c] The floor space to be provided in the quality control room [5]

33. The arrival of an aircraft at an international airport tends to follow a poisson fashion, inspite of scheduled flight time, due to high operating variability in the schedule time. It can be assumed that the aircraft arrives at an average rate of 6/hr. The landing service is provided through a single runway by a control tower according to ED with an average service time of 6 mins/fight:

[a] Find the probability that will more than 10 mins all together to wait for landing and to land an aircraft [0.513]

[b] What is the probability that the runway will be free for an incoming flight [0.4]

34. At what rate must the clerk of a super market work in order to ensure a probability of 0.9 that the customer will not have to wait longer than 12 mins on the system. It is assumed that there is a poisson fashion at an rate of 15/hr. The length is service by the clerk has an ED

[a] Also find the average number of customers queuing for service [0.738]

[b] The probability of having more than 10 customers in the system [$1.9 * 10^{3}$]

35. A mechanic is to be hired to repair a machine which breaks down at an average rate of 3/hr. Breakdowns are distributed in time in a manner that may be regarded as poisson. The non-productive time on any machine is considered to cost the company Rs. 5/hr. The company has narrowed the choice to 2 mechanics A and B. The mechanic A repairs the machines at an average rate of 4/hr and he will demand Rs. 3/hr. The mechanic B costs Rs. 5/hr and can repair the machines exponentially at an average rate of 6/hr decide which mechanic should be hired. [B]

36. A commercial bank has 3 cash paying assistants, customers are found to arrive in a poisson fashion at an average rate of 6/hr for business transaction. The service time is found to have an ED with a mean of 18 mins. The customers are processed on FCFS basis, calculate:

[a] Average number of customers in the system [2.334]

[b] Average time a customer spent in the system [0.389]

[c] Average queue length [0.532]

[d] How many hrs a week can a cash paying assistants is expected to spend with the customers? [24]

37. A super market has two girls ringing up the sales at the counters. If the service time for each customer is exponential with a mean of 4 mins and people arrive in a poisson fashion at the counters at the rate of 10/hr then determine:

[a] The probability of having to wait for service [0.17]

[b] The expected percentage of idle time for each girl [66.5%]

[c] The expected waiting time in the queue [0.0083]

38. A telephone exchange has 2 long distant operators. The telephone exchange company finds that during the load long distance calls arriving in poisson fashion at an average rate of 15/hr. The length of service is exponentially distributed with a mean of 5 mins.

[a] What is the probability that a subscriber will have to wait for hours long distant calls on the peak hour of the day? [0.4825]

[b] What is the average waiting time for the customers?

39. An insurance company has 3 clerks in the branch of people arrive with claims against the company are found to arrive in a poisson fashion at an average of 20 per 8 hrs a day. The amount of time that a clerk spends with the client is found to have in a ED with a mean of 40 mins. The clients are processed in the order of their appeareance.

[a] How many hours a week can a clerk expect to spend with their clients? [22.28 hrs]

[b] How much time on an average does a client spend in the branch office? [0.816]

40. A bank has 2 tellers working on savings accounts. The 1st teller handles withdrawals only and the 2nd teller handles deposit only. It has been found that service time distribution for depositors and withdrawals, both are exponentially distributed with mean service time of 3 mins/customer. Depositors are found to arrive in a poisson fashion with an arrival rate of 14/hr. What would be the effect on an average waiting time for the depositors and withdrawals if each teller handles both withdrawals and deposits. What would be the effect if the time would only be accomplished by increasing the service time to 3.5 mins.

(Wq_p =0.2 hr, Wq_w = 0.117 hr, Wq = 0.06428, Wq = 0.19 hr)

41. An oil company is constructing a service station on a highway. Traffic analysis indicates that customers arrival over a most of the day would approximate a poisson distribution a mean of 24 automobiles of previous studies show that on pump could service of 10 automobiles per hr, with the service time distribution approximately the negative exponential. If 3 pumps are installed.

i) What is the probability that an arrival will have to wait in line? [0.698]

ii) What is the average number of automobiles in the system? [4.61]

iii) For what % of time would the pump be idle on an average? [17.13%]

42. At a certain airport, arrivals can be taken to follow a poisson distribution inspite of schedules, due to many constraints and uncertainties. The mean time between two arrivals is 12 mins. There are 2 separate runways, one for landing and one for takeoff. The airport service time for landing flights is exponentially distributed with a mean of 8 mins per flight. When one flight is being serviced, another incoming flight cannot be cleared for landing due to safety regulations. Calculate

i) What is the chance that an incoming flight is straightaway cleared for landing? [0.33]

ii) What is the average waiting time for incoming flight to be cleared for landing? [0.267]

iii) What is the probability the waiting time is in excess of 50% of the average waiting time found in (ii)? [0.245]

iv) There is a proposal that the airport should be converted into an international terminal. One of the important requirements of the international terminal is that the average waiting time should be reduced. If an additional runway is provided with independent service facility for landings of a nature similar to the existing one, what will be the average waiting time for any air flight to be cleared for landing?

43. There are 15 computerized reservation counters at a railway station. The average time spent per customer by a booking clerk is 5 minutes. Average arrivals per hour during three types of activity periods and customer's acceptable waiting time are given below:

Types of period	Arrivals/hr	Customer's acceptable waiting time, min
Peak	110	15
Normal	60	10
Low	30	5

Determine how many counters should be kept open during each type of period.

44. A self-service store employs one cashier at its counter. Twelve customers arrive on an average, for every 5 minutes and the cashier can serve 10 customers in 5 minutes. Assuming poisson distribution for arrival rate and exponential distribution for service rate, find:

i) Average number of customers in the queue.
ii) Average number of customers in the system.
iii) Average time a customer spends in the system.
iv) Average time a customer waits before being served, and
v) Probability of the queue size being greater than or equal to the number of customers.

45. Arrivals at a tool crib are poisson distributed at an average rate of 6 per hour. The service time at the tool crib is exponentially distributed with a mean time of 0.05 hour. Determine: (i) the probability that the arriving person at the tool crib has to wait; (ii) the average number of persons at the tool crib; (iii) the average length of queue that forms from time to time; (iv) the average time spent by the person in the tool crib; (v) the average time shunt by a person waiting in the queue.

8

Project Management Problems

INTRODUCTION

Management of big projects with a large number of activities pose complex problems in planning, scheduling and controlling, especially when the activities have to be performed in a specialized technological sequence. Fortunately, two operation research techniques, PERT (Program Evaluation and Review Technique) CPM (Critical Path Method) are available to assist the project manager in carrying out these responsibilities. These techniques make heavy use of networks to help plan and display the coordination of all the activities. They also normally use a software package to deal with all the data needed to develop schedule information and then to monitor the progress of the project.

Project management software such as MS Project is widely available for these purposes. Some recent surveys report that as much as 70% of the world's mathematical programming problems can be represented by network related models. The applications of networks are:

- Determination of the shortest route between two cities in a network of roads.
- Determination of the time schedule for the activities of a construction project.
- Determination of the time schedule from oil fields to refineries through a pipeline network.

The solution of these situations and it is accomplished through a variety of network optimization algorithms. The following are the algorithms:

- Minimal spanning tree
- Shortest route algorithm
- Maximum flow algorithm
- Minimum cost network algorithm

PERT & CPM has been used for a variety of projects, including the following types:

1. Construction of a new plant
2. Research and development of a new product
3. Movie production
4. Relocation of a major facility
5. Installation of a management information system
6. Conducting an advertising campaign.

PERT & CPM were independently developed in the late 1950s ever since they have been among the most widely used OR techniques.

Project Management Problems

Exercises problems on **PERT and CPM**

1. A project has the following characteristics. Construct the PERT network, number the nodes by Fulkerson's rule. Find the estimated time to complete the project, calculate total float, free float and independent float. What is the probability that project will be completed in 35 days.

Activity	Predecessor activity	Most optimistic time	Most likely time	Most pessimistic time
A	—	6	9	18
B	—	5	8	17
C	A	4	7	22
D	A	4	7	10
E	B	4	7	16
F	B	2	5	8
G	C,E	4	10	22

2. The project consists of seven activities, whose time estimates are listed below.

Activity	1-2	1-3	1-4	2-5	3-5	4-6	5-6
Optimistic Time (weeks)	1	1	2	1	2	2	3
Most likely time (weeks)	1	4	2	1	5	5	6
Pessimistic Time (weeks)	7	7	8	1	14	8	15

i) Draw the network and identify the critical path.
ii) Find expected duration and variance for each activity.
iii) Calculate length and variance of critical path.
iv) Determine the probability that project will be completed no more than four weeks later than expected time.
v) Determine the probability that project will be completed no more than four week.

3. The following table lists the jobs of a network along with their time estimates.

	Duration in days		
Jobs	**Optimistic**	**Most likely**	**Pessimistic**
1-2	3	6	15
2-3	6	12	30
2-4	5	11	17
3-4	3	9	27
3-5	1	4	7
5-6	2	5	8
3-6	4	19	28
4-6	2	5	14

i) Draw the network and calculate the length and variance of critical path.
ii) What is the probability that jobs on critical paths will be completed by the due date of 40 days?
iii) What is your estimate of the probability that the entire project will be completed by due date?

4. Consider the network of the following figure.

The normal and crash points for each activity are given in the table. Find the different minimum crash schedule (32 days schedule) that can occur between normal and crash times.

Activity	Normal duration	Normal cost	Crash duration	Crash cost
(1,2)	20	2000	15	3000
(1,3)	10	1500	7	2400
(2,5)	15	1000	10	1500
(3,4)	16	3000	12	4000
(3,5)	22	4500	16	5700
(4,5)	14	1500	10	2100

5. The following table lists the jobs of a network with their time estimates.

Job	Duration in days		
	Optimistic	**Mostly likely**	**Pessimistic**
1-2	3	6	15
1-6	2	5	14
2-3	6	12	30
2-4	2	5	8
3-5	5	11	17
4-5	3	6	15
6-7	3	9	27
5-8	1	4	7
7-8	4	19	28

i) Draw the project network.
ii) Calculate the length and variance of the critical path.
iii) What is the probability that the jobs on critical path will be completed by 24 days?

6. A project consists of the activities as given in the following table:

Activity	Immediate predecessor activity	Time in wks		
		t_o	t_p	t_l
a	-	1	7	1
b	a	1	7	4
c	-	2	8	2
d	b,c	1	1	1
e	c	2	14	5
f	a,c	2	5	8
g	d	3	6	15

i) Draw the project network.
ii) Identify the critical path and determine the expected completion time of the project.
iii) What is the probability that the project would be completed within 17 weeks.

7. The details of a small project are given in the following table:

Activity	Immediate predecessor (s)	Duration (weeks)
A	-	2
B	-	6
C	-	4
D	B	3
E	A	6
F	A	8
G	B	3
H	C,D	7
I	C,D	2
J	E	5
K	F,G,H	4
L	F,G,H	3
M	I	2
N	J,K	5

i) Determine an activity on arrow diagram to represent the project.
ii) Compute early start, early finish, late start, late finish, total float and free float for each activity. Present the answer in tabular form.
iii) What is the critical path and project duration?

8. A project consists of seven activities. The table below givens the estimates of the optimistic, most likely and pessimistic duration in weeks of each activity.

Activity	Estimated Duration in Weeks		
i-J	Optimistic	Most Likely	Pessimistic
1-2	1	1	7
1-3	1	4	7
1-4	2	2	8
2-5	1	1	1
3-5	2	5	14
4-6	2	5	8
5-6	3	6	15

i) Draw project network.
ii) Compute the expected duration and variance of each activity.
iii) Determine the expected project duration and its variance.
iv) What due date has about 90% chance of being met ?

9. Draw the network diagram, identify the critical path and compute total and free floats for the following projects:

Activity	Immediate Predecessor	Duration (Weeks)
a	-	8
b	a	9
c	b	7
d	a	15
e	c,d	4
f	e	1
g	d	4
h	e,g	5
i	h,f	4

10. The following table represents various data of a project:

Task	Immediate predecessor	Duration (days)	Variance (days)	Crash data: Maximum compression (days)	Crash data: Expediting cost per day (Rs.)
A	-	6	2	0	-
B	A	2	0	1	50
C	B	12	3	2	80
D	A	8	1	2	175
E	A	7	2	1	100
F	C,D	16	4	0	-
G	D	23	2	1	100
H	E,D	25	5	3	300
I	F,G,H	4	1	1	1,000

a) Find the critical path and slacks.
b) Find the probability of completion within 45 days.
c) Find the minimum project duration and the expected cost increase.

11. Given the following data, compute the following:

i) The earliest and latest expected time to reach each node.
ii) The probabilities that each task will be completed on schedule.
iii) The expected task time and variance for each job and for the entire project.

Job	Predecessor	O	M	P	Scheduled completion time (in days)
A	-	8	10	14	20
B	-	14	20	26	25
C	A,B	16	20	22	40
D	A,B	24	30	36	80
E	C	28	36	46	80
F	D,E	18	20	21	100

12. Draw the network and find the critical path and project duration for the following project.

Job	Duration (in days)
A	13
B	5
C	8
D	10
E	5
F	6
H	10
I	6
J	5
K	4
L	12

13. The utility data for a network is given below. Crash the network to minimum project duration and determine the total cost of the project for that duration. The indirect cost is Rs. 6000 per day determine the optimum project schedule.

Activity	Normal duration (days)	Normal cost (Rs.)	Crash duration (days)	Crash cost (Rs.)
0-1	1	5,000	1	5,000
1-2	3	5,000	2	12,000
1-3	7	11,000	4	17,000
2-3	5	10,000	3	12,000
2-4	8	8,500	6	12,500
3-4	4	8,500	2	16,500
4-5	1	5,000	1	5,000

14. Draw a network for job production:

Activity	Preceded by	Time (weeks)
A	-	15
B	-	15
C	A	3
D	A	5
E	B,C	8
F	B	12
G	E	3
H	E	14
I	D,G	3
J	F,H,I	12

i) Determine the critical path.

ii) Calculate total slack and free slack for non-critical activities.

15. The following table lists the jobs of a network with their time estimates.

Jobs	Duration on the days		
i-J	t_o	t_m	t_p
1-2	3	6	15
1-6	2	5	14
2-3	6	12	30
2-4	2	5	8
3-5	5	11	17
4-5	3	6	15
6-7	3	9	27
5-8	1	4	7
7-8	4	19	28

Determine the probability that the jobs on critical path will be completed within a due date of 41 days.

16. Construct the network diagram comprising the activities A, B, …. And L, such that the following relationships are satisfied:

i) A, B and C are the first activities of the project and can start simultaneously.

ii) A and B proceed D.

iii) B proceeds E, f and H.
iv) F and C proceed G.
v) E and H proceed I.
vi) C, F and I proceed K.
vii) D proceeds L.
viii) L, G and K are terminal activities of the project.

17. The three time estimates for the various activities of a project are given below:

Activity	Time (a, b, m)	Activity	Time (a, b, m)
(1, 2)	(1, 4, 3)	(4, 5)	(10, 15, 12)
(1,3)	(5, 8, 7)	(4, 7)	(8, 12, 10)
(1, 4)	(6, 9, 7)	(5, 6)	(7, 11, 8)
(1, 6)	(1, 3, 2)	(5, 7)	(2, 8, 4)
(2, 3)	(3, 5, 4)	(6, 7)	(5, 7, 6)
(2, 5)	(7, 9, 8)		
(3, 4)	(10, 20, 15)		
(3, 7)	(12, 14, 13)		

i) Draw the project network
ii) Find mean and variable of each activity duration
iii) Find the critical path and expected duration of the project
iv) What is the probability that the project will be completed in 35 units of time?

18. The table below shows the jobs, their normal time and cost, crash time and cost for a project. Indirect cost is Rs. 300 per day.

Activity	Normal cost in Rs.	Normal duration (days)	Crash cost in Rs.	Crash duration (days)
1-2	1400	6	11900	4
1-3	2000	8	2800	5
2-3	1100	4	1500	2
2-4	800	3	1400	2
3-4	-	0	-	-
3-5	900	6	1600	3
4-6	2500	10	3500	6
5-6	500	3	800	2

a) Draw the network and indicate the critical path.
b) What is the normal duration and cost of the project?
c) If all the activities are crashed what will be the duration and cost?
d) What is the optimum duration and minimum project cost?

19. Determine the early start, early finish, late start, late finish, total float, free float for all the activities that form a project given below. Duration in days for each activity (I, j) is also given in the table. Identify the critical path.

Activity	Duration
(0, 1)	2
(0, 2)	3
(1, 3)	2
(2, 3)	3
(2, 4)	2
(3, 4)	0
(3, 5)	3
(3, 6)	2
(4, 5)	7
(4, 6)	5
(5, 6)	6

20. Consider a project consisting of nine jobs (A, B,…., I) with the following precedence relation and time estimates (in days)

Job	Predecessors	Optimistic time	Most-likely time	Pessimistic time
A	-	2	5	8
B	A	6	9	12
C	A	6	7	8
D	B,C	1	4	7
E	A	8	8	8
F	D,E	5	14	17
G	C	3	12	21
H	F,G	3	6	9
I	H	5	8	11

i) Determine the average (expected) time and variance for each job.
ii) Determine the critical path and expected duration of the project.
iii) Show critical path on the network.
iv) What is the probability that the project will be completed within 50 days?

21. Consider a project consisting of the following jobs.

Job	Predecessor	Time (days)
A	-	15
B	-	10
C	A,B	10
D	A,B	10
E	B	5
F	D,E	5
G	C,F	20
H	D,E	10
I	G,H	15

i) Draw the arrow diagram and determine the critical path.
ii) Determine early start time, late time, early finish time and late finish time for each job.
iii) Calculate the total slack for each job.

22. The following table provides the estimates of time and costs for different activities of a project.

Activity	Normal time (weeks)			Cost (Rs.)	Crash time (weeks)	Crash cost (Rs.)
	a	*m*	*b*			
1-2	1	3	5	15,000	1	19,000
2-3	1	4	7	18,000	3	24,000
2-4	1	3	5	14,000	2	16,000
2-5	5	8	11	15,000	7	16,000
3-6	2	4	6	13,000	2	15,000
4-6	5	6	7	12,000	4	13,600
5-7	4	5	6	20,000	4	24,000
6-7	1	3	5	17,000	1	20,600

The normal delivery time is 16 weeks for a contract price of Rs. 1,24,000/-. Based on computed profitability for each of the following schedules, recommend the delivery schedule for the project.

Contract delivery time (weeks)	Contract amount (Rs.)
15	1,42,500
14	1,45,000
13	1,50,000
12	1,52,500

23. The details of a project are given as under:

Activity	Immediate Predecessors	Time (days)		
		t_o	t_m	t_p
A	-	25	30	45
B	-	10	15	20
C	-	20	25	35
D	A	5	3	5
E	C	5	7	12
F	B	1	1	1
G	D,F	4	5	7
H	D,F	2	2	3
I	E,F	4	4	6
J	H,I	8	10	14
K	G,J	6	8	15

i) Draw the network diagram.
ii) Find the critical path.
iii) Find the slacks for each activity.
iv) Determine the probability
   1) That the project gets completed before 54 weeks.
   2) The project takes more then 70 weeks to get completed.

24. The details of normal time, normal costs and crash time, crash costs for a project are as given below.

Activity	Normal Time (weeks)	Normal Cost (Rs.)	Crash Time (weeks)	Crash Cost (Rs.)
1-2	2	500	1	800
1-4	5	900	3	1300
1-3	4	800	3	1000
2-4	1	400	1	400
3-4	3	1200	2	1800
4-5	6	700	4	900
3-5	8	600	4	1200

The indirect project costs are as given below.

Project duration (weeks)	9	10	11	12	13
Indirect cost (Rs.)	6000	6150	6200	6500	7100

a) Find the total cost of finishing the project in 9, 10, 11, 12, and 13 weeks.

b) Find the least cost duration in weeks.

c) Plot a graph of duration vs. total project costs.

25. A project consists of the following activities with precedence relationships as shown.

i) Draw the project network.

ii) Find the critical path.

iii) Determine the total float and free float of each activity.

Job	Predecessor	Time (weeks)
A	-	3
B	-	6
C	A	2
D	A,B	4
E	A	2
F	C	7
G	B,C	4
H	C,E	3

26. From the data given below, construct the network and number the nodes using Fulkerson's rule.

Calculate the expected task times and their variance. Carrying out the forward pass computation and backward pass computation, find T_E and T_L for all nodes.

Task	A	B	C	D	E	F	G	H	I	J	K
Least time (days)	4	5	8	2	4	6	8	5	3	5	6
Maximum time (days)	8	7	12	7	10	15	16	9	7	11	13
Most likely time (days)	5	7	11	3	7	9	12	6	5	8	9

Precedence Relationship : A, C, D can start simultaneously. E > B, C; F, G > D; H, > E, F; J > I, G; K > H; B > A. Also determine:

i) Critical path

ii) Probability of completing the project in 40 days.

Duration of the project if the probability of completion = 0. 816.

27. The following table gives that the activities in a construction project and other relevant information

Activity	1-2	1-3	2-3	2-4	3-4	4-5
Duration	20	25	10	12	6	10

i) Draw the network for the project.

ii) Find critical path.

28. The following table gives the activities in a construction project

Activity	Normal Time (Days)	Crash Cost Rs.	Normal Cost Rs.	Crash Cost Rs.
1-2	20	17	600	720
1-3	25	25	200	200
2-3	10	8	300	440
2-4	12	6	400	700
3-4	5	2	300	420
4-5	10	5	300	600
4-6	5	3	600	900
5-7	10	5	500	800
6-7	8	3	400	700

Determine the optimum time and the cost by crashing the relevant activities.

29. A project consists of 12 jobs labeled A to L. The order in which the jobs are to be carried out are: Job A comes first and precedes B, C and D. Both B and C must be done before E starts, and C and D must precede F, G and H can start as soon as D is completed. Jobs succeeds E, F and H can start as soon are completed. Job L comes after J and K.

i) Draw the arrow diagram for the project using as few dummies as possible.

ii) Number the nodes using Fulkerson's rule.

30. A small project has the following time and cost estimates:

Job	Immediate Predecessor	Normal		Minimum	
		Time (Hrs)	Cost (Rs.)	Time (Hrs)	Cost (Rs.)
A	—	8	80	6	100
B	A	7	40	4	94
C	A	12	100	5	184
D	A	9	70	5	102
E	B,C,D	6	50	6	50

The overhead costs are Rs. 25 per hour. Compute the minimum cost project schedule.

31. For a project whose details are given below, find normal duration and cost optimum duration and cost schedule. Indirect cost works at Rs. 70 per day.

Task	Activity	Normal		Crash	
		Time	Cost	Time	Cost
1	A – B	8	100	6	200
2	A – C	4	150	2	350
3	B – D	2	50	1	90
4	B – E	10	100	5	400
5	C – D	5	100	1	200
6	D – E	3	80	1	100

32. As a project manager of a company you are involved in a PERT network for laying the foundation. The relevant information for all the activities of this project are given below.

Activity	Time to weeks			Normal cost for expected duration Rs.	Crash cost Rs.	Immediate predecessor
	t_o	t_m	t_h			
A	2	3	4	6,000	8,000	-
B	4	5	6	12,000	13,500	A
C	3	5	7	16,000	22,000	A
D	2	4	6	8,000	10,000	A
E	1	2	3	6,000	7,500	C, D
F	1	3	5	14,000	20,000	B, E

Construct the PERT network for the project and determine the expected duration of the project.

There is a penalty clause at the rate of 2,500 Rs. for every week or part thereof exceeding seven weeks. With the crashing costs given above determine the optimal duration of the project to minimize the sum of the project cost and penalty cost.

33. Table below shows jobs, their normal time and cost and crash time cost for a project.

Job	Normal		Crash	
	Time (days)	Cost (Rs.)	Time (days)	Cost (Rs.)
1-2	6	1400	4	1900
1-3	8	2000	5	2800
2-3	4	1100	2	1500
2-4	3	800	2	1400
3-4	Dummy	-	-	-
3-5	6	900	3	1600
4-6	10	2500	6	3500
5-6	3	500	2	800

Indirect cost for the project in Rs. 300 per day.

i) Draw the network of the project.

ii) What is the normal duration cost of the project?

iii) If all activities are crashed, what will be the project duration and corresponding cost?

34. As a project manager of a company you are involved in a PERT network for laying the foundation. The relevant information for all the activities of this project are given below.

Activity	Time (weeks)			Normal cost for expected duration Rs.	Crash cost Rs.	Immediate predecessor
	t_o	t_m	t_h			
A	2	3	4	6,000	8,000	-
B	4	5	6	12,000	13,500	A
C	3	5	7	16,000	22,000	A
D	2	4	6	8,000	10,000	A
E	1	2	3	6,000	7,500	C, D
F	1	3	5	14,000	20,000	B, E

i) Construct the PERT network for the project and determine the expected duration of the project.

ii) There is a penalty clause at the rate of Rs. 2,500 for every week or part thereof exceeding seven weeks. With the crashing costs given above determine the optimal duration of the project to minimize the sum of the project cost and penalty cost.

35. A CPM network has the following activity time and cost data:

Activity	Normal time	Crash time	Cost slope
1-2	5	2	Rs. 40
1-3	4	1	Rs. 50
1-6	6	6	-
2-3	3	2	Rs. 70
2-5	5	4	Rs. 40
3-4	3	1	Rs. 25
4-5	4	4	-
4-7	2	1	Rs. 80
5-7	5	1	Rs. 200
6-7	5	3	Rs. 90

a) Draw the network and identify critical path.

b) Crash the net activity step by step until the shortest duration is reached.

36. Table below shows jobs, their normal time and cost and crash time cost for a project.

Job	Normal		Crash	
	Time (days)	Cost (Rs.)	Time (days)	Cost (Rs.)
1-2	6	1400	4	1900
1-3	8	2000	5	2800
2-3	4	1100	2	1500
2-4	3	800	2	1400
3-4	Dummy	-	-	-
3-5	6	900	3	1600
4-6	10	2500	6	3500
5-6	3	500	2	800

Indirect cost for the project in Rs.300 per day.

i) Draw the network of the project.

ii) What is the normal duration cost of the project?

iii) If all activities are crashed, what will be the project duration and corresponding cost? Find the least cost project schedule 21.

37. The matrix below gives the precedence relationship and duration of activities (5 * 4) in a project.

Precedence	Duration	Following Activity								
Activity	In days	A	B	C	D	E	F	G	H	I
A	15					1	1			
B	18			1	1					
C	22							1	1	
D	12					1	1			
E	16							1	1	
F	17									1
G	4									1
H	27									
I	19									

a) Draw the network.

b) Label the nodes as per Fulkerson's rule.

c) Determine the critical pates and it's duration.

d) What is the total slack for each activity?

38. Construct the arrow diagram for the activities given below satisfying the relationship.

i) A, B and C have no predecessor activity and can start simultaneously.

ii) A and B precede D.

iii) B precedes E, F, and H.

iv) F and C precede G.

v) E and D precede I.

vi) I, H and G are terminal activities of the project.

If the duration of the activities respectively are,

A = 2 hours, B = 3 hours, C = 1 hour, D = 4 hours, E = 7 hours, F = 5 hours, G = 4 hours, H = 12 hours and I = 7 hours, determine the critical path by calculating the earliest and latest event times.

39. Draw the network and number the events and find out critical path, total floats and free float for each activity.

Activity	Immediate predecessor	tE (days)
A	-	5
B	A	4
C	-	7
D	B,C	3
E	B	4
F	D,E	2

40. The following table gives the activities in a construction project and other relevant information.

Job	Normal (days)	Normal cost (Rs.)	Crash (days)	Crash cost (Rs.)
1 – 2	6	1400	4	1900
1 – 3	8	2000	5	2800
2 – 3	4	1100	2	1500
2 – 4	3	800	2	1400
3 – 4	-	-	-	-
3 – 5	6	900	3	1600
4 – 6	10	2500	6	3500
5 – 6	3	500	2	800

If indirect costs are Rs. 300/day, find:

1) Draw the network and find out project duration.
2) What is the minimum length of the project?
3) Find the optimum duration and optimum project cost.

41. A certain project consists of the following activities:

a) A and B can start simultaneously and each of them takes 10 days to finish.

b) C can start after A is halfway through whereas D can start after 4 days of progress of A.

c) D also requires 3 days of progress on C and 6 days of progress on B for its commencement.

d) E can commence after A is finished and B is halfway through.

e) C, D and E take 6, 8 and 12 days of execution time.

   i) Construct the network and identify the critical segments of the task/s.

   ii) Find the minimum time required for completion. If 3 days extra time is made available, what will be floats on each of the jobs/segments of jobs?

42. The maintenance job of an heat exchanger follows the following schedule:

	Task	Precedence	Duration
A	Dismantling pipelines		10 hours
B	Dismantling ends	A	25 hours
C	Dismantling of tube bundle	B	12 hours
D	Cleaning of bolts	B	10 hours
E	Cleaning tube bundle	C	15 hours
F	Cleaning of shell	C	5 hours
G	Cleaning of heads	A	6 hours
H	Replacing of tube bundle	E,F	5 hours
I	Replacing ends	H	4 hours
J	Prepare the shell for pressure test	I	25 hours
K	Prepare tubes for pressure test	I	15 hours

Draw the CP network, find earliest start and finish and latest start and finish time for each task. Identify the critical path.

43. A project consists of a tasks labelled A, B, C,… H, I with the following relationship, (w < x, y means x and y cannot start until w is completed: x, y, < w means w cannot start until both x and y are completed)

A < D, E; B D < F; C < G; B < H: F, G < I

Construct the network diagram having the above constraints. Find also the minimum time of completion of the project when the time (in days) of completion of each task in as follows:

Task	A	B	C	D	E	F	G	H	I
Task	23	8	20	16	24	18	19	4	10

44. Draw a network of the following project and number the events. Activities A and B can start at the beginning of the project. When A is computed, C and D can start. E can only start when B and D are finished. F can start when B, C and D are completed and is the final activity. The following table given the list of jobs, their normal duration and cost, and the crash duration and cost.

Job	Normal		Crash	
	Duration (day)	Cost (Rs.)	Duration days	Cost (Rs.)
1-2 ----------	1	25	1	25
2-3 ----------	3	80	2	140
1-3 ----------	5	125	3	225
3-4 ----------	3	100	2	175
4-5 ----------	1	30	1	30

Calculate the necessary information for the project.

45. A project schedule has the following characteristics:

Activity	Time	Activity	Time
1-2	4	5-6	4
1-3	1	5-7	8
2-4	1	6-8	1
3-4	1	7-8	2
3-5	6	8-10	5
4-9	5	9-10	7

i) Construct PERT network.

ii) Find critical path of the project, total flat, free float, and independent float of each activity.

46. Explain early event time and late event time.

47. The following table gives the activity time data of a certain project together with IMMEDIATE predecessor requirements:

Activity	Immediate	Time in days
A	-	3
B	-	4
C	A	2
D	B	3
E	A,B	5
F	C,D	3
G	E	4
H	F,G	2

Construct the network for the project and find the critical path and hence the time required to complete the project. Find also free float for all the jobs.

48. Write short notes on any four of the following:

a) Characteristics of a DPP.
b) Ordering and carrying costs.
c) Saddle points games.
d) Two person zero sum game.
e) PERT and CPM.
f) Floats in networks.

49. In the following table optimistic, most-likely and pessimistic times are respectively shown against each connected activity from 10 to 100 in a project. Find the critical path by constructing a network. The scheduled completion time for the project is 48 days. Calculate the probabilities of finshing the project within this time (given that 89.5% probability corresponds to a normal deviation of + 1.25)

Activity	Times	Activity	Times
10-20	4,8,12	20-30	1,4,7
20-40	8,12,16	30-50	3,5,7
40-60	0,0,0	40-60	3,6,8
50-80	3,6,9	50-80	4,8,6
60-100	4,6,8	70-90	4,8,12
80-90	2,5,8	90-100	4,10,16

9

Game Theory Problems

INTRODUCTION

Life is full of conflicts and competition. The examples of conflict includes parlour games, military battles, political campaigns, advertising and marketing campaigns by competing business firms and etc. Game theory deals with decision situation in which two intelligent opponents have competing objectives.

In a game conflict, two opponents known as players will each have a number of alternatives or strategies. Associated with each pair of strategies is a pay-off that one player pays to the other, such games are known as two-person zero sum games because the gain by one player equals the loss of the other so that the sum of their net winning is zero. The basic characteristics of two-person zero sum games consider the game called odds and evens. In general a two-person game is characterized by

1. The strategies of player 1
2. The strategies of player 2
3. The pay-off table.

A primary objective of game theory is the development of rational criteria for selecting a strategy. The following two key assumptions are made:

1. Both players are rational
2. Both players choose their strategies solely to promote their own welfare.

Game theory contrasts with decision analysis where the assumption is that the decision maker is playing a game with a passive opponent which choose its strategies in some random fashion.

Applications:

- Constant sum TV game
- Odds and evens
- Coin toss game with bluffing
- Prisoner's dilemma
- Advertising prisoner's dilemma game
- Chicken game.

Game Theory Problems

1. Solve the following game, use dominance method to reduce the matrix, write the strategies adopted by each player and value of game.

	B_1	B_2	B_3	B_4	B_5
A_1	4	4	2	-4	-6
A_2	8	6	8	-4	0
A_3	10	2	4	10	12

2. Solve the following game, use graphically method. Write the strategies adopted by each player and value of game.

	b_1	b_2	b_3
a_1	6	4	3
a_2	2	4	8

3. Reduce the following game by dominance and find the game value.

		Player B			
		I	**II**	**III**	**IV**
	I	3	2	4	0
Player A	II	3	4	2	4
	III	4	2	4	0
	IV	0	43	0	8

4. Use graphical method to solve the following game.

		Player B	
		1	**2**
Player A	1	1	2
	2	5	6
	3	-7	-9
	4	-4	-3
	5	2	1

5. Solve the game with the following payoff matrix.

		Player B				
		1	**2**	**3**	**4**	**5**
Player A	1	6	15	30	21	6
	2	3	3	6	6	4
	3	12	12	24	36	3

Write down the optimal solution for both the players and the value of the game.

6. Solve the following game with pay-off matrix of A given in the table below.

		Player B	
		1	**2**
Player 'A'	1	-2	0
	2	3	-1
	3	-3	2
	4	5	-4

7. Players A and B play a game in which each player has three coins (20p, 25p and 50p). Each of them selects a coin without the knowledge of the other player. If the sum of the values of the coins is an even number. A wins B's coin. If the sum is on odd number, B wins A's coin.

i) Develop a pay-off matrix with respect to player A.

ii) Find the optimal strategies for the players. What is the value of the game?

8. A solve the following game graphically.

		Player B	
		1	2
	1	1	2
	2	5	6
Player A	3	-7	-9
	4	-4	-3
	5	2	1

9. Find the range of p and q that will render the entry (2,2) a saddle point in the following game.

	Player B		
	1	q	6
	p	5	10
A	6	2	3
	6	5	10

10. Solve the following game graphically

		Player B	
		1	2
	1	2	4
A	2	2	3
	3	3	2
	4	-2	6

11. Using relation of dominance or otherwise solve the game whose pay-off matrix is given below.

		Player Y (Pure strategy)		
		1	2	3
	1	0	-2	2
Player X	2	5	4	-3
Pure Strategy	3	2	3	-4

Find the optimal mixed strategy for player X and Y.

12. Solve the game graphically given the pay-off matrix as follows:

		Player B		
		1	2	3
Player A	1	1	3	12
	2	8	6	2

Where y, - - - and x, - - - are the probability associated with B and A respectively.

13. Solve the game whose pay-off matrix is given below

		Player B			
		I	II	III	IV
Player A	I	3	2	4	0
	II	3	4	2	4
	III	4	2	4	0
	IV	0	4	0	8

14. The following matrix represents the pay-off to P_1 in a rectangular game between two persons P_1 and P_2.

8	15	-4	-2
19	15	17	16
0	20	15	5

By the notion of dominance, reduce the game to 2×4 game and then solve it graphically.

15. Use dominance rule to reduce the following game to either $2 \times n$ or $m \times 2$ game and then solve it graphically.

		B			
		B_1	B_2	B_3	B_4
A	A_1	19	6	7	5
	A_2	7	3	14	6
	A_3	12	8	18	4
	A_4	8	7	13	-1

16. Solve the game for the pay-off matrix of two persons zero sum game.

		B	
		B_1	B_2
A	A_1	-6	7
	A_2	4	-5
	A_3	-1	-2
	A_4	-2	5
	A_5	7	6

17. Use the dominance principle and solve the following game:

1	-3	-2
0	-4	2
-5	2	3

18. Solve the following game using graphical method:

3	-1	0
2	1	-1

19. Solve the following game problem graphically:

1	2
5	4
-7	9
-4	-3
2	1

20. Use the relation dominance to solve the rectangular game whose pay-off matrix to A is given below.

	1	2	3	4	5	6
1	0	0	0	0	0	0
2	4	2	0	2	1	1
3	4	3	1	3	2	2
4	4	3	7	-5	1	2
5	4	3	4	-1	2	2
6	4	3	3	2	2	2

21. Given a normal distribution with mean 40 and SD 6, find the value of x that has.

a) 45% of the left area and 39.25

b) 14% of the area to the right and 46.48 b. Use the relation dominance to solve the rectangular game whose pay-off matrix to A is given below.

	1	2	3	4	5	6
1	0	0	0	0	0	0
2	4	2	0	2	1	1
3	4	3	1	3	2	2
4	4	3	7	-5	1	2
5	4	3	4	-1	2	2
6	4	3	3	2	2	2

22. Solve the following 2*3 game by method of sub games

		1	2	3
A	1	-1	7	6
	2	5	-3	3

23. Solve the following game by drawing network, critical path and find pay-off matrix.

		B		
		1	2	3
	1	2	-2	2
A	2	-2	-2	6
	3	-2	+4	-2

24. Explain the criterion of dominance of strategy in a game.

25. The following gives the pay-off matrix of a certain game:

	Pure strategy
Player X	1
	2
	3

Player Y		
1	2	3
0	-2	2
5	4	-3
2	3	-4

Find the optimal mixed strategies for players X and Y.

26. Explain the salient characteristics of a Queue system.

27. Trucks line up at a highway weigh bridge facility according to a poisson arrival pattern with a mean arrival rate of 12 per hour. The average time taken to attend on a truck follows an exponential distribution with an average time of 4 min per truck. Find:

i) The average queue length of trucks.
ii) The % utilization of the weigh bridge.
iii) The average time required for a truck to wait and get serviced.

28. Two players independently select one of mouse, cat, tiger and elephant and simultaneously reveal their choices it is known that the cat chases the mouse (for scorre 1), the tiger chases the cat (for score 2), the elephant chases the tiger (for score 3) and the mouse chases the elephant (for score 4). All other combinations yield a zero score. Formulate the pay-off matrix and determine the optimal strategies of the two players.

	Mouse	Cat	Tiger	Elephant
Mouse	0	-1	0	4
Cat	1	0	-2	0
Tiger	0	2	0	-3
Elephant	-4	0	3	0

29. Two players A and B match coins. If the coin matches, then A wins one unit of value, if the coins do not match then B wins one unit of value. Determine optimum strategies for the players and the value of the game.

30. A and B each take out one or two matches and guess how many matches opponent has taken, if one of the players gueses correctly then the looser has to pay him as many rupees as the sum of the numbers held by both players. Otherwise, the payout is zero. Write down the pay-off matrix and obtain the optimal strategies of both players.

31. In a game of matching coins with two players, suppose A wins one unit of value when there are two heads, wins nothing when there are two tails and loses ½ unit of value when there are one head and one tail. Determine the pay-off matrix, the best strategies for each player and the value of the game to A.

32. Consider a modified form of matching biased wins game problem. The matching player is paid eight rupees if the two wins turn both heads and one rupee if the wins turn both tails. The non-matching player is paid three rupees when the two wins do not match given the choice of being the matching or non-matching player, which one would you choose and what would be your strategy?

33. The pay-off matrix for a 2-person,zero-sum game is given:

Starting the criterion you adopt, find the optimum strategies for two players when stating the criterion you adopt, find the optimal strategies for two players when a, b, and c are all of the same sign. What simplifications are effected for the case, when a, b and c are not of the same sign? What is the value of the game in either case?

		Player A		
		I	II	III
	I	a	0	0
Player B	II	0	b	0
	III	0	0	c

34. Two items of value Rs. 100 and Rs. 130 are to be auctioned at a public sale. Only two bidders are interested in these items. Bidder A has Rs. 100 available and bidder B has 80 available. What should be their strategies? If each bidder is interested in maximizing his own gain.

35. Consider a modified form of matching biased coins game problem. The matching player is paid Rs. 8 if the two coins turn both heads and the player is paid Rs. 3 when the two coins do not match. Given the choice of being the matching or non-matching player, which one would you choose and what should be your strategy.

10

Replacement Problems

INTRODUCTION

Replacement problems fall into two categories depending upon the use pattern of the equipment involved i.e. whether the equipment wear out or becomes obsolete with time or suddenly fails. The problem is to balance the cost of new equipment against the cost of maintaining efficiency on the old and loss in efficiency. The problem is to determine which item to replace and how often to replace, so as to minimize the sum of the following cost:

- Cost of equipment.
- Cost of replacing the unit.
- Cost associated with failure of the unit, loss of earnings due to equipment breakdown.

All industrial and military equipment sets work with time and usage of it functions with decreasing efficiency, for example, a machine requires higher operating cost, a transport vehicle like car or aeroplane requires more and more maintenance cost, a railway time table becomes more and more obsolete with the passage of time. Increasing repair and maintenance cost necessitates the replacement of the equipment.

The replacement policy consists of calculating the increased operating cost, maintenance cost, forced idle time cost together with cost of the new equipment.

A separate but similar problem involves the replacement of small value items such as electric bulbs, radio tubes etc., of equipment which does not deteriorate with time but suddenly fails. The objective is to minimise the sum of the cost of the item, cost of replacing the item and the cost associated with failure of item.

The equipment needs replacement not because it no longer performs to the designed standards, but because more modern equipment performs higher standards. The replacement problem has the following three techniques:

- Replacement of items that deteriorate, that is, whose maintenance costs increase with time.
- Replacement of items whose maintenance and repair costs increase with time, ignoring charges in the value of money during the period.
- Replacement of items whose maintenance costs increase with time and value of money also changes with time.

The replacement situations may be placed into four categories:

- Replacement of capital equipment that becomes worse with time.
- Group replacement of items that fail completely.
- Problems of mobility and staffing.
- Miscellaneous problems.

Replacement Problems

1. Machine 'A' costs Rs. 9000, annual operating costs are Rs. 2000 for first year and then increases by Rs. 2000 every year. Determine the best age to replace the machine. There is a machine 'B' which costs Rs. 10,000, annual operating costs are Rs. 400 for first year and then increases by 800 every year. Owner has a machine of type 'A' which is one year old, should he replace with 'B', if so when?

2. A computer contains 10,000 resistors. When any resistor fails, it is replaced. The cost of replacing a resistor individually is Re. 1.00. If all the replaced at the same time, the cost per resistor would be reduced to 35 paise. The percentage of survival at the end of month 't' is given below:

Month	0	1	2	3	4	5	6
% surviving at end of month	100	97	90	70	30	15	0

What is the optimum replacement plan. At what group replacement price per resistor would a policy of strictly individual replacement become preferable to adopted policy.

3. The following mortality rates have been observed for a certain electric bulb.

Week	1	2	3	4	5	6	7	8
% failure by end of week	5	13	25	43	68	88	96	100

There are 100 bulbs in a factory and it costs Rs. 4.00 to replace an individual bulb which has burnt out. If all bulbs were replaced simultaneously, it would cost Re. 1 per bulb. It is proposed to replace all bulbs at fixed intervals whether or not they are burnt out and to continue replacing burnt out bulbs as they fail. At what intervals should all the bulbs be replaced.

4. The following mortality rates have been observed for a certain type of electric bulbs.

Week	1	2	3	4	5	6
Prob. of upto end of week	0.09	0.25	0.45	0.85	0.97	1.0

There are a large number of such bulbs which are to be kept in working order. If a bulb fails while in service, it costs Rs. 30/- to replace that individual bulb. On the other hand, if all the bulbs are replaced simultaneously it would cost Rs. 7/- per bulb. Determine replacement policy.

5. An electric equipment contains 500 resistors. When any resistor fails, it is replaced. The cost of replacing a resistor individually is Rs. 20. If all the resistors are replaced at the same time, the cost is Rs. 5 per resistor. The percentage of resistors surviving, S(i) at the end of month i is given in table below.

Percent survival rate

Month i	0	1	2	3	4	5
S(i)	100	90	75	55	30	0

Determine the optimum replacement policy among the following:

- Replace the resistors individually when they fail.
- Replace all resistors simultaneously at fixed intervals and replace individual resistors as and when they fail in service during the fixed interval. If the second one is optima, then find at what equal intervals should all the resistors be replaced.

6. The following mortality rates have been observed for a certain type of light bulb.

Week	1	2	3	4	5	6
% Survival by the end of week	90	85	60	35	20	0

There are 1,000 bulbs in use, and it costs Rs. 4.5 to replace an individual bulb which has burnt out. If all bulbs were replaced simultaneously; it would cost Rs 1.25 per bulb. Is individual replacement policy economical? If decided to go for group replacement what should be the best interval.

7. A machine cost Rs. 9000. Annual operating cost in the first year is Rs. 200 and then increased by Rs. 2000 every year. Determine the best age at which to replace the machine? If the optimum replacement policy is followed, what will be the average yearly cost of owning and operating the machine.

8. A car owner finds from past records that the maintenance cost per year of the car whose purchase price is Rs. 80,000/- are as given below:

Year	1	2	3	4	5	6	7	8
Maintenance cost in Rs.	1000	1300	1700	2200	2900	3800	4800	6000
Resale price in Rs.	40,000	20,000	12,000	6,000	5,000	4,000	4,000	4,000

Determine the time at which it is profitable to replace the car.

9. The following data has been estimated for a piece of equipment that costs Rs. 60,000/-.

Year	1	2	3	4	5	6	7	8
Maintenance cost in Rs.	10,000	10,100	1,200	10,300	10,400	10,500	10,600	10,700
Resale price in Rs.	1,000	1,100	1,300	1,700	2,700	2,800	3,500	4,700

If money is worth 10% when should the equipment be replaced.

10. A decorative series lamp set circuit contains 10,000 bulbs. When any bulb fails it is replaced. The cost of replacing bulb individually is Re. 1/- only. If all the bulbs are replaced at the same time the cost per bulb would be reduced to 35 paise. The percent surviving S(t) at the end of the month and S(t) the probabilities of failure during the month t are given below.

t	0	1	2	3	4	5	6
S(t)	100	97	90	70	30	15	0
P(t)	—	0.03	0.37	0.20	0.40	0.15	0.15

What is the optimal replacement plan?

11. Based on historical data, the annual maintenance cost and resale price of a machine whose purchase price was Rs. 15,000 are as follows:

Year	1	2	3	4	5	6	7	8
Maintenance cost in Rs.	2500	3000	3500	4500	5700	7000	8500	10000
Resale price (Rs.)	7500	3800	1900	1000	500	300	200	200

Compute the optimum replacement age.

12. The initial cost of an item is Rs.15,000 and maintenance costs for different years are given below:

Year	1	2	3	4	5	6	7
Running cost Rs.	2,500	3,000	4,000	5,000	6,500	8,000	10,000

Find the replacement policy of the capital is worth 10% and no salvage value.

13. The following mortality rates have been observed for a certain type of electric bulb.

Week	1	2	3	4	5	6	7	8
% failure by the end of the week	5	13	25	43	68	88	96	100

There are 1000 bulbs in a factory and it costs Rs. 10/- to replace an individual bulb. If all bulbs are replaced simultaneously it would cost Rs. 2.5 per bulb. Compare the group replacement and individual replacement policies.

14. The following mortality rates have been observed for certain type of light bulbs.

Week	1	2	3	4	5
% of failing by end of week	10	25	50	80	100

There are 1000 bulbs in use, and it costs Rs. 2/- to replace an individual bulb which has burnt out. If all bulbs were replaced simultaneously, it is proposed to replace all bulbs at fixed intervals, whether or not they have burnt out, and to continue replacing burnt out bulbs as they fail. At what intervals should all the bulbs be replaced? Briefly explain the situations when the replacement is to be done.

15. A truck owner finds from his past records that the purchase price is Rs. 8,000/-. The maintenance cost and resale price are given below:

Year	Maintenance cost (Rs.)	Resale price (Rs.)
1	1,000	4,000
2	1,300	2,000
3	1,700	1,200
4	2,200	600
5	2,900	500
6	3,800	400
7	4,800	400
8	6,000	400

Determine at which time it is profitable to replace the truck if the money is worth 10% per year.

11

Inventory Management Problems

INTRODUCTION

Inventory theory has evolved through several stages since it began in the 1920s. A business or an industry usually maintains a reasonable inventory of goods to ensure smooth operation. The real live inventories facing many people was to manage an enormous variety of items with enough interrelations among items to pose a management problem. To maintain the data processing has oriented subject called inventory management or inventory control evolved. The major concern was for organising and maintaining records rather than optimizing performance.

An inventory can be defined as any idle resources of an enterprise. Inventory models are classified into two categories:

- Deterministic models.
- Stochastic models.

Many companies in other parts of the world also have been revamping the way in which they manage their inventories. The application of operations research techniques in this area (sometimes called inventory management) is providing a powerful tool for gaining a competitive edge. How do companies use operations research to improve their inventory policy for when and how much to replenish their inventory? They use scientific inventory management comprising the following steps:

1. Formulate a mathematical model describing the behaviour of the inventory systems.
2. Seek an optimal inventory policy with respect to this model.
3. Use a computerized information processing system to maintain a record of the current inventory levels.

4. Using this record of current inventory level, apply the optimal inventory policy to signal when and how much to replenish inventory.

The following are the models:

- Purchasing model: No shortages.
- Manufacturing model: No shortages.
- Multi-item deterministic model.
- Purchasing model with shortages.
- Manufacturing model with shortages.
- Stochastic models.
- Purchase inventory model with price breaks.

Applications

- Manufacturing speakers for TV sets.
- Wholesale distributions of bicycles.
- Electrical appliance manufacturer.
- An aircraft company.
- Service system.
- Cement manufacturer.
- Other manufacturers.

Inventory Management Problems

1. The demand for a particular item is 18,000 units per year. The holding cost per unit is Rs. 1.20 per year and cost of procurement is Rs. 400. No shortages are allowed and the replacement is instantaneous. Determine EOQ, number of orders per year, time between orders and annual cost when of one unit is Re. 1.

2. Alpha industry needs 15,000 units per year of brought out components, which will be used in its main product. The ordering cost is Rs. 125 per order and the carrying per unit per year is 20% of the purchase price per unit. The purchase price per unit is Rs. 75. Find the economic order quantity, number of order per year and time between successive order.

3. The annual demand for an automobile component is 36,000 units. The carring cost is Re. 0.50 units/year. The ordering cost is Rs. 25.00 per order and the shortage cost is Rs. 15.00 unit/year. Find the optimal values for the following:

- Economic order quantity.
- Maximum inventory.
- Maximum shortage quantity.
- Cycle time.
- Inventory period.
- Shortage period.

4. A company uses 50,000 units of raw material per year. Raw material costs Rs. 1.2 per item. Ordering cost of items is Rs. 45 per order and item carrying cost is 15% per year of the average inventory.

- Find the economic order quantity.
- Suppose that the company follows the EOQ policy and it operates for 300 days a year, that the procurement time is 12 days and safety stock is 500 units, find the point, the maximum and average inventories.

5. A small bank is allocating a maximum of 800,000 for personal and car loans during the next month. The bank charges an annual interest rate of 14% for personal loans and for car loans. Both types of loans are repaid at the end of a one year period. The amount of car loans should be at least twice as much as that of personal loans. Past experience has shown that debts amount to 1% of all personal loans. How should the funds be allocated?

6. ABC radio company has a product for which we can have inventory model with bench order (i.e., shortages are permitted). The following information is available:

- Demand = 2000 units/year.
- Cost of each item = Rs. 50/-.
- Holding cost = Rs. 10/- per year per item.
- Ordering cost = Rs. 25/- per order.
- Back order or shortage cost = Rs. 30/- unit/year.

Find:

- Optimal order quality.
- Cycle time.
- Total cost.

7. The standard weight of special purpose brick is 5 kg and it contains two basic ingredients B_1 and B_2. B_1 costs Rs. 5/kg and B_2 cost Rs. 8/kg strength considerations dictate that the brick contains not more than 4 kg of B_1 and a minimum of 2 kg of B_2. Since the demand for the product is likely to be related to the price of the brick, find out graphically the minimum cost of the brick satisfying the above conditions.

8. An item has a demand of 9,000 units/year. The cost of one procurement is Rs. 100 and the holding cost per unit is Rs. 2.40 per year. The replacement is instantaneous and on shortages are allowed. Determine:

- The economic lot size.
- The number of order per year.
- The time between orders.
- The total cost per year if the cost of one unit is Re. 1.00.

9. Write a note on Kuhn Tucker conditions and its relevance in solving optimization problems.

10. A manufacturing firm producing refrigerators has given a contract to supply 50 units at the end of the first month, 50 at the end of the second month and 50 at the end of the third. The cost of producing refrigerators in any month is the square of the production quantity. Excess production if any can be carried forward to meet future demand at a carrying cost of Rs. 20 per item carried per month. There is no opening inventory of refrigerators. Find how should the production of refrigerators be scheduled in order to minimize the total of production cost and carrying cost.

11. Explain the different costs involved on inventory problem.

12. A company purchases certain chemicals which are required for its process. Shortages are not allowed. The demand for the chemical is 1000 kg/month. The cost of one purchase is Rs. 800/- and the holding cost for one unit is Rs. 10/- per month. The unit cost depends on the amount purchased as given below.

Amount in kg	Cost/kg
0-249	Rs. 8/-
250-449	Rs. 7/50
450-649	Rs. 7/-
650-above	Rs. 6/75/-

Determine the optimal purchasing quantity and optimal total yearly cost.

13. Explain with diagrams the fixed order quantity system and periodic review system.

14. A manufacturing company uses Rs. 75,000 worth components annually in a process. Cost per order is Rs. 45/- and the carrying charges are 25% of the average inventory. The company follows the EOQ policy. Now supplier has indicated that if the company however buys components four times a year in equal quantities, a discount of 2% off list price would be given. Would you accept the company to accept the offer? In order to maintain the present total cost, what should be the minimum discount if four orders of equal quantities are placed in a year?

15. Explain the different costs involved on inventory problem.

16. (i) M/s. TV-Assembly, needs 10,000 picture tubes/year. The cost of one procurement is Rs. 80/-. The holding cost per tube is Rs. 3.00 per year. The rush purchase of tubes, if not in stock amounts to equivalent storage cost of Rs. 6/- per tube per year. If it is instantaneous replenishment, determine how much they should order, at what interval and at what total cost?

(ii) If the company wants to reduce the holding cost to Rs. 2.40 per tube/year and the supplier manages to reduce the procurement cost to Rs. 60/- per order, what percentage reduction in penalty cost for shortage, he should negotiate so that his total associated cost of inventory is reduced by 50%.

17. You have to supply your customer with 100 units of certain product every Monday. You obtain the product from a local supplier at Rs. 60 per unit. The costs of ordering and transportation from supplier are Rs. 150 per order. The cost of carrying inventory is estimated at 15% per year of the cost of the product.

- Find the lot size which will minimize the cost of the system.
- Determine the time between orders and number of orders per year.

18. There is a contract to supply 1000 items a month at a uniform rate and each time a production run is started it costs Rs. 50/-. The cost of storing an item per month is 20 paise. The number of items to be produced per run has to be ascertained. Find out the total set-up cost and average inventory cost if the run sizes are 500, 600, 700 and 800 and comment on the result. Using the 'EOQ' formulate find out the production run size.

19. An overhead crane moves jobs from one machine to another and must be used every time a machine requires loading or unloading. The demand for services is random. Data taken by recording the elapsed time between service calls followed an exponential distribution having a mean of well over 30 minutes. In a similar manner, the actual service time of loading or unloading took an average of 10 minutes. If the machines time is valued at Rs. 8.50 per hour, how much does the down time cost per day?

20. An organization has four vendors to supply three of its subcontract items A, B and C. The vendors V_1, V_2, V_3 and V_4 have provided the quotations as per the unit price matrix shown below:

Vendors	(Unit prices of items) Items		
	A	B	C
V_1	5	4	6
V_2	6	2	8
V_3	4	4	4
V_4	1	6	3

The total quantities of items A, B and C required are 400, 600, 200 respectively. Vendors V_1, V_2, V_3 and V_4 refuse to supply orders whose quantities (all items put together) are less than 200, 150, 300 and 100 numbers respectively. However they are willing to supply more, as much customers wishes. How should the orders be placed if the company, as a policy, desires to satisfy all vendors with minimum order quantities to maintain good vendor relationships?

21. Write short notes on any four of the following:

- Two bin system of inventory control.
- Ordering and carrying costs.
- ABC analysis.
- Pure and mixed strategies in game.
- Floats in a network.
- Critical path.

22. Derive an expression for the economic ordering quantity when:

A = Annual demand.
B = Ordering cost.
C = Carrying rate Rs./Re. inventory per year.
E = Unit cost of the item.

23. A certain material with an annual consumption of 6,000 kg involves an ordering cost of Rs. 200 per order. The carrying rate is 20% p.a. The unit cost of the material is Rs. 2,000 per kg. Shortages are deemed prohibitively costly. Find EOQ.

12

Sequencing Problems

INTRODUCTION

If there are n jobs which require processing on some or all of m different machines. The effectiveness can be measured for any given sequence of jobs at each machine and the most suitable sequence of jobs at each machine and the most suitable sequence is to be selected among all theoretically possible sequences. It is always possible to select the best sequence by testing each one. It is practically impossible because of large number of computations.

Suppose there are n jobs (1, 2, 3,.....n) each of which has to be processed one at at time at each of m machines a, b, c,..... the order of processing each job through machines is given for ex, job 1 is processed through machines is A, C, B- in this order. The time that each job must require on each machine is known. The main aim is solve the problem with perfect sequence for processing the jobs so that the total elapsed time for all the jobs will be minimum.

The following terminology and notations will be used:

- Number of machines
- Processing order
- Processing time
- Idle time on a machine
- Total elapsed time
- No passing rule

Principal assumptions:

1. No machine can process more than one operation at a time.
2. Each operation, once started must be performed till completion
3. A job is an entity.
4. Each operation must be completed before any other operation.
5. Time intervals for processing are independent of the order in which operations are performed.
6. There is any one of each type of machine
7. A job is processed as soon as possible subject to ordering requirements.
8. All jobs are known and are ready to start processing before the period under considerations begin.
9. The time required to transfer job between machines is negligible.

Sequencing Problems

1. Determine the optimal sequence of jobs that minimizes the total elapsed time required to complete the following jobs and find the total elapsed time the jobs are to be processed on three machines M_1, M_2 and M_3 in the order M_1, M_2, M_3.

	A	B	C	D	E	F	G
M_1	3	8	7	4	9	8	7
M_2	4	3	2	5	1	4	3
M_3	6	7	5	11	5	6	12

2. Determine the minimum elapsed time for completing the following two jobs. Also determine the sequence of jobs on each machine. Processing times and the sequence of operations are given below:

Job 1	:	A-5	to	C-3	to	D-6	to	E-4	to	B-3
Job 2	:	A-3	to	D-8	to	C-4	to	B-2	to	E-6

3. A maintenance crew of a certain factory is divided in 3 groups. Group 'A' inspects the machine breakdown and write the case sheet. Group B certifies the repairs and hands it over to the production manager after test run. Group C undertakes actual repairs on machine at a given time. Eight machines are under breakdown and estimated time values for 3 groups are as follows. Determine the best sequence to repair the machines and the corresponding time.

Machine	**1**	**2**	**3**	**4**	**5**	**6**	**7**	**8**
Group A	3	5	7	4	3	6	2	4
Group B	7	6	5	9	8	6	5	10
Group C	1	2	4	3	5	3	2	2

4. Find an optimal solution to an assignment problem with the following cost matrix.

		Jobs			
		J_1	J_2	J_3	J_4
Machines	M_1	10	9	7	8
	M_2	5	8	7	7
	M_3	5	4	6	5
	M_4	2	3	4	5

5. A machine shop has six machines: A, B, C, D, E and F. Two jobs must be processed through each of these machines. The time spent on each machine and the sequence of the jobs through these machines are:

Order	: 1	2	3	4	5	6	7
Job I :	A-20	C-10	D-10	B-30	E-25	F-15	—
Job II :	A-10	C-30	A-10	B-15	D-10	F-15	E-20

Solve graphically to find the order of the jobs to be done on each of the machines in order to minimize the total time necessary to finish the jobs.

6. Use graphical method to minimize the time needed to process the following jobs in machines shown below. Calculate the idle time, total elapsed time and find which job must be processed first on each of the machines.

Job 1:	Seg/Time	A - 1	B - 3	C - 4	D - 3	E – 2
Job 2:	Seg/Time	A - 5	B - 2	D - 2	C - 2	E - 1

7. Find the optimal sequence for the following sequencing problem of four jobs and five machines when passing is not allowed. The processing times are given below.

	Machines				
Job	A	B	C	D	E
1	7	5	2	3	9
2	6	6	4	5	10
3	5	4	5	6	8
4	8	3	3	2	6

8. Find the sequence that minimizes the total time required in performing the following jobs on three machines in the order C,B,A.

		Jobs						
	1	1	2	3	4	5	6	7
Machines	2	8	7	6	9	10	10	9
	3	3	4	5	2	1	1	6
	4	8	3	7	2	5	5	1

9. Five jobs are to be processed through three machines A,B,C in the order ACB. The processing times are shown below. Find the sequence of jobs and total elapsed time.

		Jobs				
		1	2	3	4	5
Machines	A	4	9	8	6	5
	B	8	10	6	7	11
	C	5	6	2	3	4

10. Determine the optimal sequence of jobs which minimizes the total clasped time "T" based on the following information.

	Processing Time in Hours				
Job No.	**1**	**2**	**3**	**4**	**5**
Machine A	5	7	6	9	5
Machine B	2	1	4	5	3
Machine C	3	7	5	6	7

Also calculate minimum elapsed time.

11. Determine the minimum elapsed time for the two jobs for which detail of processing times and sequence of operation are as given below:

Job 1:	A-6	to	C-7	to	B-5	to	D-4	to	E-5
Job 2:	A-4	to	B-3	to	C-5	to	E-2	to	D-4

12. The time spent on processing of two jobs on six machines A, B, C, D, E and F and the technological sequence for processing two jobs on the machine and the processing time in minutes are as follows:

Job 1:	A-15	C-10	D-12	B-25	E-25	F-15
Job 2:	A-10	C-30	B-15	D-15	F-10	E-20

Determine the minimum elapsed time processing the jobs and also determine the sequence of jobs on each machine.

13. Determine the minimum elapsed time for completing the following two jobs. Details of processing times in minutes and the sequence of operations are given below:

Job 1:	A-4	to	C-3	to	D-6	to	E-4	to	B-2
Job 2:	C-6	to	A-4	to	D-4	to	B-3	to	E-2

Also determine the sequence of jobs on each machine.

14. Two jobs are to be processed in 6 machines, A, B, C, D, E and F. The technological order for these jobs on machines and the processing times for each job on machines are as follows:

Job 1:	A-3	to	B-4	to	C-2	to	E-3	to	D-2	to	F-3
Job 2:	C-3	to	B-5	to	A-4	to	D-3	to	F-4	to	E-4

15. There are five jobs each of which to be processed through three machines A, B and C in the order BCA. Processing time in hours are:

Job	A	B	C.
1	7	3	4
2	9	8	5
3	5	7	1
4	6	5	2
5	10	4	3

Determine the optimum sequence for the five jobs and the minimum elapsed time.

16. A book binder has one printing machine, one binding machine and one finishing machine. The time in minutes required for printing, binding and finishing operations for each book are known, determine the order in which the books should be processed in order to minimize the total time required to process all the jobs. Find the total time required.

Book	1	2	3	4	5
Printing time	40	90	80	60	50
Binding time	50	60	20	30	40
Finishing time	80	100	60	70	110

17. Find the sequence that minimizes the total elapsed time required to complete the following jobs on the three machines M_1, M_2, M_3 in the order M_1, M_2, M_3.

	A	B	C	D	E
M_1	3	8	7	5	2
M_2	3	4	2	1	5
M_3	5	8	10	7	6

18. Determine the minimum elapsed time for two jobs for which details of processing times and sequence of operation are as given below:

Job 1:	A-7	to	B-4	to	C-6	to	D-5	to	E-4
Job 2:	A-3	to	B-8	to	C-4	to	E-1	to	D-5

19. Two jobs to be processed on four machines A, B, C and D. The technological ordering for these jobs on machines are as follows:

Job 1:	A	B	C	D
Job 2:	D	B	A	C

Processing times are given in the following table:

	Machines			
	A	B	C	D
Job 1:	4	6	7	3
Job 2:	4	7	5	8

Find the optimal sequence of jobs for each machine.

20. Find the sequence that minimizes the total elapsed time required to complete the following tasks:

Tasks	A	B	C	D	E	F
Time on first machine	2	5	4	9	6	6
Time on second machine	6	8	7	4	3	9

21. Determine the minimum elapsed time for completing the following two jobs. The technological sequence and the processing times are given below:

Job 1:	A-2	B-4	C-6	D-8	E-4
Job 2:	C-4	A-3	B-5	D-7	E-3

22. The time spent in processing two jobs for five machines and the prescribed technological order are as follows:

Job 1:	A-2	B-3	C-5	D-2	E-1
Job 2:	D-6	C-2	A-3	B-1	E-3

Determine the minimum time elapsed and the sequence of jobs on each machine.

23. The time spent in processing of two jobs on six machines A, B, C, D, E and F the necessary technological ordering of machines are as follows:

Job 1:	A-20	C-10	D-10	B-30	E-25	F-15
Job 2:	A-10	C-10	E-15	D-10	F-15	E-20

Use graphical method to determine an optimal sequence of jobs which minimizes the total elapsed time. Also determine which job is first done on each of the machines.

24. The time spent in processing of two jobs on six machines A, B, C, D, E and F and the necessary technological ordering of machines are as follows:

Job 1:	A-20	C-10	D-10	B-30	E-25	F-15
Job 2:	A-10	C-10	E-15	D-10	F-15	E-20

25. The time spent in processing two jobs on five machines and the necessary technological order are as follows:

Job 1:	A-1	B-3	C-4	D-3	E-2
Job 2:	A-5	B-2	D-2	C-2	E-1

Determine the minimum elapsed time and also determine the sequence of jobs on each machine.

26. Time spent on processing two jobs on five machines and the necessary technological order are as follows:

Job 1:	A-2	B-3	C-4	D-3	E-1
Job 2:	A-1	C-2	B-2	D-2	E-7

Determine the minimum elapsed time and also the sequence of jobs on each machine.

27. Determine the minimum elapsed time for completing two jobs. Details of processing times and sequence of operation are given below:

Job 1:	A-4	to	C-2	to	D-6	to	E-3	to	B-2
Job 2:	C-8	to	A-3	to	D-4	to	B-2	to	E-3

Also determine the sequence of jobs on each machine.

28. A company has eight large machines which receive preventive maintenance. The maintenance team is divided in two crews A and B. Crew A takes the machine power and replaces the parts according to a given maintenance schedule. The second crew resets the machine and puts it back into operation. At all times the no-passing rule is considered to be in effect. The serving times for each machine are given below:

	Machines							
	a	b	c	d	e	f	g	h
Crew A:	5	4	22	16	15	11	9	4
Crew B:	6	10	12	8	20	7	2	21

Determine the optimal sequence of scheduling the factory maintenance and minimum elapsed time.

29. Determine, graphically, the minimum time needed to process the following jobs on the machines shown.

		Machines				
Job 1:	Sequence:	A	B	C	D	E
	Time:	2	3	4	6	2
Job 2:	Sequence:	C	A	D	E	B
	Time:	4	5	3	2	6

30. There are six jobs to be processed on two machines and the processing times are as shown below. What is the optimum schedule assuming each job must be processed on machine. A prior to processing on machine B.

		Processing time (minutes)					
Job		1	2	3	4	5	6
Machine	A	8	6	5	7	3	8
Machine	B	4	7	5	4	6	3